Daniel Filmus is a Member of Parliament, Mercosur, a Citra/Conicet Researcher, and Professor of the University of Buenos Aires.

Presidential Voices of Latin America

Daniel Filmus

Translated by Benjamin Jabiu

Revised edition

Critical, Cultural and Communications Press
London
2017

CONTENTS

To my parents.
To Marisa, Malena and Maite

Latin America is a region of the world where you find everything you look for. Lucky for us that we are that way — like that nonsense that somebody brought to me one time from the summit of science. They asked me: what does a Negro from Haiti have in common with a gaucho from La Pampa? But of course they have something in common! They do not know it, but they have something for sure. Why? Because both of them have been condemned to the amnesia of an official story sick with racism, maleness, elitism and militarism. They are mutilated in the acknowledgment of what we were — in the shared memory — and mutilated, too, in the awareness of the reality. But as this begins to crack open, as we begin to crack it open, as we begin to be what we can be — which is an infinite wide and splendid thing — we will discover that there are a lot more points in common than we suppose, beginning with the most obvious one, that has to do with the common-sense duty to defend ourselves together.

Eduardo Galeano
Pueblos magazine, December 2005

Acknowledgments

Presidential Voices is an extended translation of *Presidentes: Voces de América Latina* (Buenos Aires: Aguilar, 2010). The present publication arose from the EU project "MEMOSUR: Lessons for Europe from Argentina and Chile" under Professor Bernard McGuirk's (slightly different!) Presidency of the International Consortium for the Study of Post-Conflict Cultures. I am especially grateful to Bernard for translating the new Prologue to this revised edition.

My thanks to everyone who pitched in with ideas, effort and enthusiasm so that this project and this book could become a reality, especially to Tristán Bauer, Ignacio Hernaiz, Jessica Tritten, Marcos Sacchetti, Pablo Santangelo, Diva Da Matta and all the people at Occidente Producciones.

To Inés Tenewicki, Fabiola Carcar y Mariana de la Fuente. To Diego Tomasi.

To Canal Siete (Channel 7), Canal Encuentro, Horizontal Property Workers Union (SUTERH), Argentine Union of Private Teachers (SADOP), Credicoop Bank, TELECOM, Sangari Foundation, Organisation of Ibero-American States (OEI), and UNESCO.

This reprint of *Presidential Voices* is published at a very particular juncture of the history of Latin America. The region is going through a retraction of power on the part of popular governments. Neoliberal counter-offensives, beginning with *coups d'état* in Honduras and Paraguay, have been reinforced by the electoral success of the right in Argentina, the gentler *coup d'état* in Brazil, the current crisis in Venezuela, the defeat in the referendum for re-election in Bolivia and the difficult electoral situation in Ecuador. The offensive for the restoration of conservative governments has deployed new methods of seeking to undermine the consolidation of processes of change across the region. The joint actions of the powerful media, sectors of the corporate judiciary and of concentrated capital have managed to weaken and halt the progress of a substantial part of the said processes of change. What is more, in spite of having advanced through an important period of growth led by the grouping of governments strongly committed to change, Latin America seems not to have found the way to keep moving forward towards a model that complements economic development and social justice. It has returned in recent years to reveal its self as vulnerable to the conditions of international markets and, especially, to the price of raw materials, factors which have weakened its economy and thrown into question the possibility of continuing with national, popular and progressive policies. All this has led to a sharp reversal that finds many of our countries going back to applying neo-liberal formulae that, in the nineteen nineties, ended up in unemployment, inequality, poverty and political chaos.

It is obvious that a neo-liberalism which seeks to reclaim the initiative does not cater for new proposals for the region. It reiterates those that have already failed and led our countries into deep crisis. The governments of Michel Temer and Mauricio Macri demonstrate the limitations of the right in finding strategies that might allow the growth of the country and an improvement in the living conditions of the people. Their principal objective is to tear down the achievements and the rights obtained in the last decade and to restore the logic of that concentration of riches that ruled throughout the nineteen nineties.

Many of the presidents interviewed in this book headed the transformative processes in their own countries. Some of them attained the presidency after long years of leadership of struggle and political militancy, as in the case of the Partido dos Trabalhadores (PT) in Brazil and the Frente Grande in Uruguay, while others came to power in more or less unexpected ways. For the first time, a peasant, a metal worker, a bishop, two medical doctors, two women, a descendant of native peoples, a physicist, rose to power and responsibility for the political conduct of our countries. Many of them had been proscribed or exiled for political reasons and had participated in social movements and the defence of human rights. Never before had the vital trajectories, the views and perspectives of the presidents of the region been interwoven with the histories and the realities of their peoples

To re-read these interviews today allows a measuring of the "long decade" of transformations achieved by these new national and popular governments. On the one hand, for the first time in many years, an important group of countries in the region managed to achieve an urgent economic growth with a greater distribution of wealth. This change, unusual for the previous half-century, derived from the fact that the said governments pursued non-orthodox policies in the economic and social domains. Political programmes meant affecting the interests of the privileged sectors of society and advancing in models that permitted redistributions of wealth in the direction of the historically most backward sectors of society. On the other hand, a reading of these interviews from within the current context helps us to rethink, now in a tone of self-criticism, both what was achieved and what failed and to open up an analysis not only of the advances but also of the issues still outstanding in this last decade in Latin America.

"Lula" da Silva, from Brazil; Tabaré Vazquez, from Uruguay; Cristina Fernández, from Argentina; Fernando Lugo, from Paraguay; Evo Morales, from Bolivia; Álvaro Uribe, from Colombia; Michelle Bachelet, from Chile; Rafael Correa, from Ecuador, and Hugo Chávez, from Venezuela, Oscar Arias, President of Costa Rica, and Daniel Ortega from Nicaragua, speak to us of different experiences, different realities, different peoples, but it is also possible to pick out from their words a common thread that leads us to ask whether we can speak about Latin American processes of similar characteristics and whether the future too will show common features. We certainly believe so. In this introduction, prepared for the new edition of *Presidents*, we shall attempt a synthesis of those processes lived through by the countries of the region, stressing the advances made in terms of economic growth, social equality, the democratization of civil rights and regional integration. To look at each of these processes will also help to identify the limits and difficulties of the models of socio-economic development undergone by the progressive regimes throughout the implementation of their policies. Let us now review the common characteristics of those Latin American processes that arose with the new century. Analysis of these will permit us to understand more deeply the contribution of each interviewed leader to this unprecedented historical moment lived by Latin America.

1. The full force of democratic institutions

One of the common features of the Latin American transformative processes has been respect for democratic systems. As distinct from the experiences of the nineteen seventies, the impact of dictatorships throughout the continent generated a profound consciousness of the need for the political, economic and social changes to occur in a context of the full application of democratic institutionalism. This is no minor issue if we take into account, as we have pointed out, the fact that many of these transformative processes have arisen from the deep crisis of legitimacy in the representation of the people and of political parties; a crisis that in a number of cases (Argentina, Venezuela, Bolivia amongst others) unleashed situations of violence and the danger of breakdown of constitutional order. Perhaps the most emblematic case is that of the access to government of the first leader of the period, Hugo Chávez (1999), elected after having attempted to take power through a military uprising in 1992. In contrast, on numerous occasions, progressive governments were those that had had to confront attacks on institutionality. Some were successful, as in Honduras (2009) and Paraguay (2012) and, more recently, Brazil (2016). In these cases, through spurious mechanisms linked to the power of the Legislature or the Judiciary and with the strong support of the dominant media, conservative forces managed to bring down the presidents under the cover of apparent democratic continuity. Evo Morales, Hugo Chávez and Rafael Correa suffered various attempts at institutional breakdown. In all these cases, strong popular mobilization, combined with the immediate reaction of the presidents and of regional organizations, prevented different types of attempted *coups* from succeeding in bringing them down. The new regional institutions, led by the Common

Prologue

Market of the South (Mercosur) and the Union of South American Nations (Unasur), played a preponderant role in these processes, based on the unanimous approval in each of these organizations of *Cartas Democráticas* that strongly sanction those countries in which a breakdown of institutional order occurs. The parliamentary attack, supplemented by the judiciary or the media, that provoked the resignation from power of Dilma Rousseff, also falls into the category of "soft" or "blank" *coups,* that the neoliberal conservative offensive attempts to impose in the region with the objective of destabilizing and bringing down progressive governments.

2. The State again has a role in applying the development model
The reconstruction of a strong and active State, able to lead the processes of change, was one of the main challenges for the new governments of the region. This implied a profound shift in the structures and the role to be played by the State, but it also demanded a profound cultural change in respect of the people's attitude towards the State itself. The destruction of the very developmental State that had led the processes of growth in Latin America in the post-war period was one of the central aims laid down by the Washington Consensus in order to apply the politics of the market and deregulation. With that aim in view, there came about a thoroughgoing delegitimizing of the role of the State in society. As some authors have argued, the neo-liberal governments of the final decades of the twentieth century were determined to transform the state of well being into a state of ill being, costly, inefficient, bureaucratic and regressive, aided and abetted by the mass media that contributed strongly to delegitimizing the State in the face of public opinion. Whence the dismantling and privatization of the roles played by the State and performed throughout the nineteen nineties with a high degree of legitimacy and social consensus.

A decade later, the enormous crisis that spelt out the failure of the market as regulator of the economic and social order allowed for the task of reconstruction to be carried out with a growing social consensus regarding the need to recuperate its historic role. The absence of State not only generated the destruction of the productive sectors in many countries of the region, with resulting unemployment and poverty, but also and at the same time prevented access to public policies of social protection for those who were left marginalized from the workings of the economy.

The recuperation of the role of the State occurred on the basis of the need for participation in the running of the development process and of the redistribution of income and benefits generated by the said development. A previous requirement was the recovery of credibility in the State's capacity to serve the common good. In this sense, an outstanding role was played by the confidence of the people in leaders who rose to power in governments that oversaw this new era, all of which was translated into an important re-legitimizing of the State. Thus, as outlined in a recent publication, we can sustain that "at present, and as distinct from in previous decades, there exists throughout the region a greater consensus regarding the role of the State as decisive at the point of guaranteeing the public good, dynamizing growth, stimulating productive development, intervening in regional development and promoting egalitarian politics to consolidate civil rights and create consensus around fiscal pacts with redistributive effects" (Bárcena and Prado, 2016)

One of the central aspects of the new role of the State was linked to its recovering the role of economic agent on the basis of nationalizations and state ownerships of businesses of vital importance in strategic sectors of the economy. This enabled the accomplishing of a triple objective: appropriating the possibility of directing development; recovering national sovereignty in decision making; and granting to the State an important part of the national wealth in order to direct it towards public investment in social programmes.

Another indicator of the growth in the role of the State in the development model is the important growth in public expenditure that allowed greater capacity to dynamize the economy, to favour growth and generate new sources of employment via public works. At the same time, and following a cyclical tendency, social spending grew strongly. This growth had shown a slight expansion throughout the nineteen nineties, but it culminated with a no less slight reduction at the outset of the new century. In this way, public spending as a percentage of the GDP was 25% in 1992-1993 and fell to 24.5% for 2002-2003. From that date on, public spending grew to 29.2% for 2010-2011.

3. Priority in growth of the internal market and employment
As we have suggested, another common feature of those Latin

American countries that achieved growth with the redistribution of wealth was the attempt to change the pattern of growth favouring the development of a productive model more centred on the generation of jobs and the internal market. Without a doubt, the favourable conditions of external financing and the rise in the prices of exportable prime materials played a fundamental role in the advantageous process lived through by the region's countries. However, these factors do not in themselves explain the transformations achieved. The policies of stimulating industrialization and of adding value through technological innovation and internal demand, though incomplete, enhanced access to consumption for great sections of historically marginalized populations. At the same time, in many cases, they allowed upward social mobility towards the middle class for important sectors that had been living in poverty (Quenan, 2014). These measures were accompanied by policies specifically destined to protect registered employment and reverse the process of flexibility and labour deregulation that had ruled in the nineteen nineties.

In contrast with what had happened in the previous decade, when economic growth was accompanied by a constant increase in unemployment and informal work, in the period 2003 to 2014 the increase in the GDP produced a steep rise in the levels of employment and formal work. In the nineteen nineties, unemployment in the region rose from 7.5% to almost 12%. In the last decade, in contrast, the percentage of the unemployed fell almost by half.

Furthermore, this change of direction in the growth model, the limitations of which we shall go on to analyze, also granted the possibility of confronting the consequences of the global financial crisis that happened from 2008. As distinct from countries in other parts of the world, Latin American states demonstrated a high degree of resilience at the level of economic growth, managing financial situations and sustaining the living conditions of the population. As Carlos Quenan has argued, "Latin America avoided a deeper recession and managed to face international turbulences without falling into a monetary or destabilizing financial crisis thanks to a reduction in the causes of vulnerability during the growth phase that began in 2003".

4. Advances in the fight against poverty and inequality
The challenge of inequality is the most important one faced by the

government of the region. It is well known that Latin America is not the continent with the deepest poverty, but it does suffer from the highest levels of inequality in the world. The active role of the State has been fundamental in converting this problem into one of the dominant topics on the agenda of public policy making. From the beginning of the twenty-first century new conceptions of equality began to emerge, incorporating different perspectives on the role of the State, including the view that it ought to guarantee a complete focus on citizens' rights, not restricted to the institutional right to vote. Human, economic, social and cultural rights come to greater prominence as much in the legislatures of each of the countries of the region as in the economic and social policies.

In respect of inequality, there was also an important change in comparison with the tendency towards growth that had been a constant in preceding decades. Studies based on the Gini coefficient show that inequality had been reducing significantly in fifteen of the seventeen countries of the region in the period from 2002 to 2011. Of course, the reduction of the levels of inequality was not homogeneous between the different countries in the different sub-periods. Between 2002 and 2008, the rate of fall in inequality was of more than 1% annually in Argentina, Brazil, Peru, Venezuela and Uruguay. Paradoxically, the drop in inequality occurred more evidently from 2008. Uruguay, Bolivia, El Salvador, Argentina and Ecuador, among others, show a more marked reduction on the Gini coefficient in this period.

In almost all cases, the reduction of inequality is much more linked to job creation, to the improvement of salaried incomes and to the role of the state in social public investment in areas such as education, health and social provision than to direct fiscal action through the redistribution produced by non-positive action. The possibility of progressive tax reform of broader scope is still pending.

Synthesizing, despite persistent social debts, advances in respect of inequality in Latin America have been substantial. As CEPAL has indicated, growth, with greater emphasis on social action and greater equity in the distribution of wealth, has meant a strengthening in social citizenship. In this realm, the first decade of the twenty-first century was one of gain for Latin America. This progress is to be valued especially at a time when the majority of countries worldwide are showing tendencies towards ever more regressive wealth distribution. Thus, the CEPAL study concludes that Latin America, a region traditionally backward in this respect, has begun to close the gap that has separated it from more developed nations.

5. Extension of human rights and new forms of democracy

The extension of rights in respect of gender, ethnicity and race in the first decade or so of the century in Latin America was substantial in almost every case, albeit with different pace and rhythm in the respective countries.

Regarding women, the achievements were very important. They achieved absolute parity of access at the different levels of education systems, with the result that nowadays the school experience does not reflect gender gaps. In the case of higher education, for instance, as distinct from in other regions of developing countries, the difference is slightly in favour of women. 23.5% of women and 21.5% of men are matriculated at this level. It is however possible to claim that the greatest inequalities of gender in the educational sphere are linked to the types of professional careers involving women at a relatively less valued level in market terms.

As far as access to the world of work is concerned, the gaps have been reduced, although far from achieving the levels of equality of the education system. In the last fifteen years, the participation of women in labour markets increased from 40% to 53%. The proportion of women with no income fell from 42% in 2002 to 32% in 2011. This factor was attributable in part to the PTC. However, the unemployment index is 35% higher in the case of women who, at the same time, are more represented in the informal sector in precarious or domestic activities with lower incomes. The right to participate in politics for women has substantially improved. Many countries legislated to promote their participation in legislative and executive powers, and four of them reached parity of representation in Congress: Ecuador (2007), Bolivia (2010), Venezuela (2008) and Costa Rica (2009).

No less striking was the advance in rights related to sexual and reproductive health that, in many cases, was incorporated in the Constitution. None the less, in a few countries (Argentina, Colombia, Costa Rica, Ecuador, Mexico and Paraguay) there is a legal limit in childhood and adolescence for the prevention of adolescent pregnancy.

Prologue

A similar phenomenon may be observed in respect of the right to sexual education. Another group benefiting from minority rights has been that of homosexuals. Almost every country adopted harsh legal penalties for gender discrimination, and some went further. Ecuador and Chile recognized civil unions between homosexuals. Argentina, Brazil and Uruguay were amongst the first countries in the world to recognize marriage between persons of the same sex. With the aim of legislating on new rights for minorities, Argentina and Brazil advanced towards guaranteeing the possibility for all citizens to decide for themselves on their sexual identity.

The extension of human rights has also been one of the prime drivers for indigenous communities. This is a population of considerable importance in the region, given that it involves about 10% in the total grouping of eight hundred native peoples recognized by States of the region. Towards the end of the nineteen eighties, Rodolfo Stavenhagen warned of the lack of recognition of indigenous rights in the great majority of the Constitutions of Latin America. At present, in only five of the twenty one Magna Carta of the region are certain rights of autochthonous peoples unrecognized. The extension of human rights implemented during the last decade, in particular in Ecuador and Bolivia, has been defined as "plurinational constitutionalism" or "dialogical and intercultural constitutionalism". Influenced by the United Nations Declaration on the Rights of Indigenous Peoples approved in 2007, these reforms arose from constituent assemblies with broad representation of the said peoples and were then ratified by referendum. Their principal characteristic is that, without questioning the unity of Nation State, it defines them as plurinational, incorporating mechanisms of political participation and specific representation of the peoples in the Legislative Assemblies.

The population of African descent also has considerable numerical importance in the region, there being some 120 million who, in the majority of cases, live in Brazil. In this case, important political measures for social integration were implemented, directed specifically at the peoples of African descent, that is to say 45% of the total. The creation of the Special Secretariat for the Promotion of Social Equality on the part of President Lula in 2003, meant to meet with the objectives established by the United Nations in the World Conference Against Racism, which took place in Durban in 2001, was a fundamental working measure taken after the equal rights legislation.

One of the principal programmes developed by the government Workers' Party (PT) concerned Diversity in the University, which sought to favour access to higher education of the most vulnerable social groupings, with emphasis on black and indigenous peoples. It is worth pointing out that the government that emerged after the so-called "soft" coup headed by Michel Temer included no minister of African descent in the cabinet. At the same time, it eliminated the Ministry of Women's Affairs, that of Racial Equality, and that of Youth and Human Rights, created by Dilma Rousseff in her period in government.

6. Strengthening of institutions and regional integration

Another common characteristic of the transformative processes of Latin America was the decision to prioritize the need for confronting common challenges in a collective manner. This determination meant deepening and modifying those perspectives out of which the processes of integration in the post-War period had been developed. Various authors defined this period as the "Fourth Wave" of Latin American integration, in an attempt to leave behind the strictly market-oriented attention that had impregnated the politics of previous decades.

The new period, which began with the coming to power of Hugo Chávez in Venezuela left its mark on the Summit of the Americas which took place in Mar del Plata in 2005. There, the principal countries of the region opted not to join the Area of Free Commerce of the Americas (ALCA) and to privilege the broadening of the decision making and the capacity for integration throughout Latin America. This approach led to a new institutionalizing of regional integration. The creation of the Bolivarian Alternative of Latin American and the Caribbean (ALBA) (2004), of the Union of South American Nations (Unasur) (2008) and the Community of Latin American and Caribbean States (Celac) (2011) are all results of this phase. Also created in 2012 was the Pacific Alliance, with the participation of Mexico, Colombia, Peru and Chile, though from a different perspective, linked in an effort to bring greater dynamism in the Asia-Pacific zone and to deepen free trade with the United States. This divergence in commercial thinking did not prevent Latin America from again demonstrating its main successes in this phase of regional integration, above all that of maintaining an important degree of cohesion in dialogue and political action. As stated at the Cochabamba

Prologue

Summit (2006): "The construction of a new model of integration cannot be based solely on commercial relations".

The creation of regional institutions to generate stronger conditions of autonomy, an increase in the level of independence in the taking of decisions at regional level – and, in particular, as a block – in multilateral organizations, the advance in the design of common strategies and traditionally neglected themes in joint form, such as defence, sustainable development and global crises, are some of the most important achievements from the political perspective of the last decade. The unity shown by Latin American countries in respect of the inclusion of Cuba in regional institutions, the opposition to interference from so-called "central" countries in our territories and the solid support for the position of Argentina with regard to the Malvinas question are examples of the agreements achieved. The possibility of intervening favourably in some of the national institutional crises and in the conflicts between member countries of the block was also important. With reference to this last point, the successful cases of intervention in the undermining of democracies in Ecuador, Bolivia and Venezuela, as well as in the bi-national conflicts such as those experienced by Colombia, Ecuador and Venezuela, contrast with the frustrations experienced by regional organizations in acting with regard to Honduras, Paraguay and, recently, Brazil. These cases demonstrate that, despite progress, there are still strong limitations to action taken in the face of democratic crises in the region.

As far as the processes of economic and productive integration are concerned, the advances made have encountered strong limitations in the structural conditions of the patterns of development. Commercial exchanges between the countries of Latin America, for example, have clearly undergone cyclical changes. This has meant that, after accompanying the tendency for growth of the economies of the region until 2008, they have stagnated since then and have even diminished in importance seen against commercial activity as a whole. However, even in the best years, commerce across the region has never exceeded 15% of the total exports. In the face of the important successes achieved in this respect at a political level and in the capacity to show a common front to the world, the reality is still distant from what has been experienced and expressed at the economic level.

7. Limits in the transformation of the production model

Until the present, we have analyzed some of the most important transformations that have led national and popular Latin American movements in the last decade. The facts demonstrate that this period saw the moment of greatest growth in forty years for Latin America. We can also observe that, for the first time in ages, these processes were associated with a series of concepts, decisions and measures which allowed economic growth to be accompanied by a better distribution of wealth and a politics aimed at creating greater social equality. The strengthening of the role of the State, the substantial lowering of the rates of poverty and indigence and a greater regional integration overall were other beneficial consequences of these processes.

Nevertheless, despite the successes achieved, what is in question today is the capacity to maintain continuity or to expand on them: "The progress made in broadening equality in the distribution of wealth is undeniable but still troubling is the sustainability of these advances, which seem to be supported more in the evolution of the economic cycle than in structural transformations" (Bárcena and Prado, 2016). The deceleration in growth that has occurred in recent years demonstrates the fragility of some of the improvements achieved and at the same time shows that Latin America today reflects still an important dependence on the production and exportation of domestic commodities. The risk of repeating longstanding behavioural patterns, including cyclical external restrictions that prevent Latin American countries from drawing on external finance and investments necessary to sustain rhythms of industrialization, is strongly in evidence.

The fall in the rate of expansion of Latin American economies over the last five years, even to the point of reaching a contraction of 0.4% of the GDP in 2015, is intimately tied to a collapse in the international price of commodities. Between 2011 and 2015, prices in agriculture and cattle-raising dropped by 30%, while as much for metals as for energy generation the fall was greater; about 50%. The impact that this process has had in terms of regional exchanges has been notable. Only for the year 2015, losses amounted to $92 billion, equivalent to 1.9% of GDP. The vulnerability of the economies of Latin America in the face of situations such as the deceleration in the world economy, in particular that of emerging markets and especially of China, has again come to the fore. The critical state of the economies of the region obliges us to

Prologue

reflect on why, despite having passed through an important period of growth led by a group of governments with a strongly transformative vocation, Latin America is again showing vulnerability to the conditions of the international market and, in particular, to commodity costs. In this context, suffice to say that the only country whose indicators separate it from other tendencies is Argentina where, whilst activities linked to the productive sector grew strongly, no less powerful was the growth in industrial activity and in services involving intensive manual labour, all of which generated at the same time a balanced growth between the internal market and exports. Manufacturing industry which, as seen, showed a growth lower than 20% in Latin America in the Argentine case showed a rise of 93%. All this meant that, contrary to what happened throughout the region, Argentina's participation in the GDP increased by almost 2%. Following on this tendency, in Argentina, there is no observable fall in manufactured goods in the total of exports. Despite this particular development, Argentina does not seem to have escaped the need to analyze critically difficulties in transforming models of production as experienced by the rest of the Latin American countries that have adopted progressive national and popular policies.

*

Returning to our protagonists, the texts which follow allow us insight into the life, the ideology, the administrations and the aspirations of those who led and continue to lead a profound transformation in the region. As recently stated by Álvaro García Linera, Vice President of Bolivia, the processes of political and social transformation are never linear, but come "in waves". The present juncture of a relative retrenchment of national and popular movements must leave some space for a new wave of deep change to the advantage of the Latin American peoples. For this process of transformation to bear fruit, and to enhance the achievements of recent years, it is necessary to learn from the successful apprenticeship we have had in overcoming the obstacles confronted and the challenges still pending. The reading of the interviews that follow will surely allow us to reach encouraging conclusions regarding our understanding of the recent past and, at the same time, our laying down paths for a future which must necessarily recuperate the best of the actions of these leaders.

Bibliography

Bárcena, A. y Prado, A. (2016). *El imperativo de la igualdad*. Buenos Aires: Cepal Siglo XXI.

Quenan, C. (2014). *América Latina y la crisis económica internacional. En Los desafíos del desarrollo en América Latina*. Paris: A Savoir, Institut des Amériques.

Stavenhagen, R. (1988). *Derecho Indígena y derechos humanos en América Latina*. México: El Colegio de México –Instituto Interamericano de Derechos Humanos.

Translation by Bernard McGuirk

This book is the result of a project that started after my participation in the inaugural meeting of the Union of South American Nations (UNASUR) that took place in the city of Brasilia in 2008.

Entering the room where the presidents were gathered, the first thing that caught my attention was the presence of women. Not many, just two. But, in a setting that had always been exclusively male, their presence was a novelty. What also caught my attention was that half of the men attending this meeting did not wear a tie — a minor but unexpected detail that suggested to me that something was causing the characteristic formality of this kind of events to crack.

As I looked at the faces of those sitting around the table, the ethnic heterogeneity was made evident. This too broke with the historical tradition. There was no doubt that one of the participants came from some native Andean-region town of ours. Three others showed features that denoted intermingling and the integration of European cultures with the natives. Furthermore, one of the participants was of African descent, and another had the characteristic features of the people from India. And thus, the picture was completed — a picture that showed that the absolute hegemony of European descent in such a high level meeting was declining.

The same looking around revealed that, for the role they were performing, it was a group of relatively young people. In fact, only two of them were over the age of 60 — an age that in another time would have been the minimum required to take part in a meeting like this.

Several of the participants who spoke made reference to their professions and previous work. Contrary to what could have been expected, lawyers were not a majority. One of them had been a farm worker and said that he had worked the land since he was a little boy. It had happened to him, not just a few times, that his family had had to endure hunger because the produce was not enough to feed them all. He had six siblings, but four of them got sick and died before the age of six. Another participant had been a metal worker, had twenty three siblings, and had to endure similar living conditions. Two other participants were doctors. The paediatrician made reference to her profession to emphasise the priority that the situation of the poorest children deserved in the debate that was taking place. The other, an oncologist, despite his new duties, kept on taking patients at least once a week. Members of the military had been present many times in meetings like this — in fact, during some decades, they were the majority. However, in this case, the only military man present had been democratically elected and a *coup d'état* had taken place in an attempt to overthrow him. As was to be expected, there were economists, but they did not seem to be the *Chicago Boys* type. One of them had got his degree from a university of the former Soviet Union. The other one, from humble origins, got the chance to go to the university thanks to a scholarship earned on academic merit. His "anti-neoliberal" language would have scared the economists that used to stand out in these sorts of meetings. Adding to heterogeneity of the professions that were present, a mathematician-physicist who had been a professor for several years took part in this meeting. Anyway, and without a doubt, the most innovative part of this event turned out to be the presence of one who until recently had served as a bishop.

The majority of those present did not come from aristocratic families, and their lives were spent away from members of the *establishment* of their respective countries. Only two of them belonged to families whose parents had graduated from universities. On the other hand, five of them had had to work from an early age to contribute to the household economy or to pay for school.

In many cases, their families had suffered from political persecution. The most serious cases included one who had seen his father imprisoned over twenty times and his three brothers tortured and expelled from their country, one who met his father at the age of five because he had been a political prisoner, and one who suffered his father's death after having endured intense torture in the prisons of the military regime of Pinochet. The fathers of two of the leaders had been murdered when they were only kids.

Most of those present in the meeting had suffered from proscription, detentions or exile for political reasons. Also, most of them had participated in social or political movements that had as their main goal to defend human rights and the living conditions of those who had less. Maybe it was because of that that they did not address each other with professional or honorific titles. No "excellence", no "doctor". Instead, it did not sound feigned to use — with complicity and even with pride — qualifying words such as *compañero*, the Spanish for

Foreword

"comrade" or "colleague".

I was stunned by what I saw and heard in this meeting. Past the stages of dictatorships and neoliberal models, Latin America was recovering its identity and, in most parts of the countries, there was a consolidation of processes that sought to combine, with original characteristics, economic growth with greater social justice.

All of these processes presupposed that regional unity was one of the most important factors for the integration — each of them with their distinctive features — to a new and fairer global political and economic order.

It was only after seeing and hearing what went on in that meeting that an idea emerged to undertake a project that could depict the moment that was taking place in Latin America and offer elements for its analysis and understanding. Never before had the life trajectories, the eyes and the perspectives of the presidents of these regions been so intertwined with the histories and realities of their people. The idea to conduct a series of interviews was thus conceived in order to give place to autobiographical stories and thoughts of the main Latin American leaders so that they could raise the key questions necessary for the understanding of the suffering, the achievements and the hopes of the inhabitants of our region.

This project was made up of participants of that first UNASUR meeting, such as: "Lula" da Silva, from Brazil; Tabaré Vázquez, from Uruguay; Cristina Fernández, from Argentina; Fernando Lugo, from Paraguay; Evo Morales, from Bolivia; Álvaro Uribe, from Colombia; Michelle Bachelet, from Chile; Rafael Correa, from Ecuador and Hugo Chávez, from Venezuela. A list to which we add the names of Oscar Arias, the President of Costa Rica — whose role in the process of pacification of Central America earned him the Nobel Peace Prize — and Daniel Ortega, President of Nicaragua — Sandinista commander and ex-guerrilla leader of the last armed revolution in the continent.

These conversations were then turned into the television series *Presidentes de Latinoamérica* (*Latin American Presidents*) that was broadcast with a vast audience through channels 7 and *Encuentro* and they will become study material for students of both high school and university levels of the region. Because of this, along with the political perspective, we sought to incorporate a sociological point of view that would open the way — with an educational intention — to inquiries on how the life stories, and the context which gave rise to these, contributed to the shaping of the ideologies and political commitments of the presidents.

Because of the conflict situation of the continent, a lot of effort was put not only into carrying out these interviews, but also into preventing the economic and political conjuncture from limiting the meetings with the presidents just to the problems of that time.

However, and contrary to what many of the people close to them had warned us about before each conversation, they all agreed to discuss personal and political matters that they had often refrained from addressing in other situations. Some delayed other commitments to expand what was being talked about. Several suggested names of friends and family to be interviewed after them in order to form a broader picture of their lives.

As some journalist friends had taught me — and as Paulo Freire used to emphasise — the key to every interview is the combination of words and silences. It was the silence right after the first answer — an answer that had been already given before — that allowed new paths to flourish in the testimonies of the interviewees. It was the silence, product of a follow-up question that never came, that many times forced the interviewees to look inside themselves for memories and thoughts at another depth. Their sincere testimonies allowed us to understand — and sometimes be moved by — the hardship and tragic reality with which their lives had been intertwined with the pain and suffering of the people and places of Latin America.

Now, those testimonies and the television programme have been turned into a book. This step, this transformation, was a pleasure to me, and a challenge too: to try and keep the freshness and emotion that the original images carried and add the context and reflection that made them richer. At the same time, the book has an added value: testimonies, anecdotes or ideas that, for television time's sake, were cut out of the series as aired.

And so, the following texts will allow us to get to know parts of the lives, ideologies, administration and dreams of the presidents that were and have been conducting a profound transformation in the region. It is my hope that these testimonies will provide tools to grasp the suffering, the struggle, the challenges and the reasons why it is possible to recover a future with greater justice and bliss for the Latin American peoples. Something is changing in the region; we must protect it.

Daniel Filmus

Argentina: Cristina Fernández
A Fearless Woman

Cristina Elisabeth Fernández was born on 19 February 1953 in Ringulet, La Plata, Buenos Aires Province. She has a younger sister, Giselle, and two children, Máximo and Florencia. She married Néstor Kirchner in 1975. She studied law at the University of La Plata, where she also began her political activism. She was Provincial Deputy of Santa Cruz between 1989 and 1995. She was a member of the Constitutional Convention of 1994 for the same province. Between 1995 and 1997 she was National Senator for Santa Cruz, and between 1997 and 2001 she was a Deputy in the National Assembly representing that district. In 2001 she went back to being a Senator, and in 2005 she was re-elected for her seat, this time for the province of Buenos Aires. On 28 October 2007, she won the Presidential Elections in the first round, with 45.29% of the votes. She was re-elected in 2011 with 54.1% of the vote.

A woman has been President of the Argentine people since 2007. Her name is Cristina Fernández, wife of Néstor Kirchner, her predecessor in office and companion in a political project of over 40 years. That woman is in her office, sitting in front of me, and I cannot resist the temptation to ask her when was the first time she thought she could become President. I tell her that many of the Presidents of the region had told me that they dreamt of that place ever since they were children. She tells me: "When I was a child, it did not occur to me to think in terms of the figure of the President. I thought about the figure of a leader, not about the institutional position in office as the President of the Republic. What I wanted was to change history, I wanted to transcend, and I wanted my journey through this world to be about more than just eating and breathing. Now, that thing about becoming President came to me later." I ask her when then, and she tells me it was only after Néstor Kirchner had come to office. And then, the conversation turns to how was it that the Kirchnerist Project came to power.

I was in my apartment in those tumultuous days of the five Presidents, in the year 2001, when Adolfo Rodríguez Saa was in office. I had the television on all day, because there were changes in the situation every minute and we wanted to know what was going on. I remember being in the kitchen and watching the television from there.

At Government House there was a microphone, and anyone who would pass by would say things, the occasional throw-away comment.

Argentina: Cristina Fernández

When one looks back at those days, one comes to think that Gabriel García Márquez could not have done a better job. That day, Néstor Kirchner came out after having talked to Rodríguez Saa. Every journalist asked him questions, and one asked him: "Are you going to run for office?" And he answered: "Yes, I will be a candidate for the Presidency." Right then I thought: "This guy has gone mad."

Néstor Kirchner ran for office in 2003, four years ahead of the plan that his political group had projected. And he got to the Presidency. According to Cristina, however, that was not the most touching moment of their political career. Cristina recounts: "The time I cried the most was when Néstor swore as Governor of Santa Cruz for the first time, in 1991. I could not stop crying when he spoke. In that moment, it seemed unbelievable for me, because Néstor had told me he wanted to be Governor of his Province back in 1976, a few days after the *coup*, and that he wanted to stay in the country and finish Law School, and then go back to his Province and become Governor. So when he finally got there, it seemed to me that he was getting to the most impressive place he could have got to in his life, because I related it to that conversation we had in 1976. And in that moment it did not even cross my mind that he could become President of the Argentine Republic."

The actual year in which Kirchnerism had planned to get to power, 2007, was actually the year in which, for the first time, a woman got to the Presidency of the Nation as head of the project. Previously, Isabel Perón had become President by accident, following the death of her husband, and there is no other precedent in the country. Not even Evita had ever had an elective office.

The questions, in this regard, are many. Is it more difficult to handle the Presidency being a woman? Must a woman in power work harder to avoid prejudice? Cristina analyses: "Gender is terrible in that seat over there. Things that nobody would ever say or do to a man are easier to say or do to a woman. Do not get me wrong, political criticism is not only acceptable, it is desired. The problem comes when people express things that have nothing to do with politics and have to do with your personal decisions regarding the clothes you wear, how you wear your hair, what you put on or what you do not put on — that is what is mediocre and silly. There are many personal discrediting remarks. It is a society that still has signs of male chauvinism, not just here, but everywhere. But I am the way I am. I have gone out to the streets covered in make-up since I was fifteen. I have always been this way and

I do not think it has to change now because I am President. I am not going to disguise myself as something I am not."

Another question that arises is if the figure of Evita is one of weight for a woman that becomes President of Argentina. Is there a special responsibility? Do you often have a sort of imaginary dialogue with her? Cristina Fernández says: "I never wanted to resemble Evita. Never. She is one of a kind and it would be silly if I tried to, and would only be a caricature. Who can resemble Evita? Nobody. She moves me — that is true — like no one else. She moves me even more than Perón did, because Eva moves you. Her life and her passion are moving. She is moving. I still see her or listen to her, and cry."

It becomes clear that Cristina Fernández does not want to be like Eva Perón, even if it is a political referent that cannot be eluded. So, which are the distinctive characteristics of Cristina as a woman in office? As if in front of an imaginary mirror, Cristina looks at herself and says: "I am very persistent with my goals. I always knew I had to get my degree in Law School and study if I wanted to move forward.

Also, whatever I do, I like it to be the best. I was like that when I was a child and I would have to draw maps for school — and still am. I want everything to be perfect, from the smallest and seemingly unimportant things to the most important ones. I have a notion that in order to get things you have to put in effort and sacrifice. When I got into office I felt an immense exercise of responsibility, but I had always felt excess of responsibility. It is what everyone who knows me says."

Cristina's mandate was marked by some adverse situations. In 2008, employers' organisations of the agricultural sector organised a strike that lasted four months, against the decision of the government to increase retentions to their exports. In addition, not two years had gone by since she was elected President when the international financial crisis exploded. I asked her, in this regard, from where she got the energies to carry on. She tells me: "My perseverance was important. I had always been persevering. And I think one has to take things as they are with dignity, without victimizing oneself. I always find strength because I also have the obligation to be strong, I have the responsibility to stay strong, and so, if I do not have the strength, I make it up. If I do not have it, I get it from somewhere, from the guts, from the stomach, from the head, from wherever I can."

Cristina's arrival at the Presidency has another overtone. Her position as woman is also relevant in a country that has had and still has the *Madres y Abuelas de Plaza de Mayo* (Mothers and Grandmothers of the Plaza de Mayo) as protagonists. The Argentine President shows her great admiration for these women who, in spite of their personal tragedies, never carried on their causes with a sense of vengeance. Cristina remembers that, in 2005, when *Obediencia Debida* (Due Obedience) and *Punto Final* (Full Stop) laws were overridden, her first reaction was to congratulate the human rights organisations, because they had always asked for compliance with the law, despite the fact that State had made their children disappear.

And she adds: "The truth is that, if I had been in their place, I do not know if I would have been so democratic in my demands. I admit it. I cannot even imagine the feelings of the people who lost their children. I cannot imagine what I would have done if they had disappeared Máximo, or Florencia, or Kirchner. I honestly do not know. Maybe I would not have been so thoughtful."

The Nuns
The encounter with Cristina Fernández had an emotional touch to it. In a room next to her office, Sister Marta Ravino, Religion teacher at La Plata's school Nuestra Señora de la Misericordia, where Cristina had studied, and Rosita Blanco, the headmistress, were waiting for her. Before meeting her, Rosita told us: "She always wore make-up. I told her that she ought to come to school with her face clean like everyone else. Marta was the one who use to clean her face, but when school was over, Cristina would grab her things and put the make-up back on." Once we had finished with the interview, Cristina met with her teachers. "You are prettier than on TV," said Marta. The three of them remembered Magdalena, a nun that, according to Rosita, abandoned the sisterhood, got married and now lives in Uruguay. "And she voted for Frente Amplio (Broad Front)," she added.

Make History — and Politics
Argentina celebrated its Bicentenary in 2010, and Cristina's office is protected by the pictures of many of those men who began to mould what we call the Motherland. You can see José de San Martín, Manuel Dorrego, Mariano Moreno, Martín Miguel de Güemes. The Argentinian President looks at them with admiration, but not with condescension. For her, there is a catch in official historiography, when it wants to make us believe those people were made of stone. "They were men and

women like each of us," she tells me. "They were not perfect. They were men and women with flaws and virtues, who smoked, had lovers, who did not want to get married, things that can also happen in the life of any individual. What is the catch? If they are presented as perfect beings, no one will identify with them, and probably no one will be able to accomplish what San Martín, Belgrano or Moreno have accomplished. They were not perfect beings, and that is what makes them valuable — because if you are perfect, doing perfect things is almost a logical consequence. But life is not like this, and history even less. On the contrary, many times, history is written with a crooked handwriting and not with the perfect, calligraphic one with Chinese ink. It is written with what it is at hand, sometimes with ink, sometimes with a pencil, and sometimes with blood, of course.

When speaking about historical processes and facts, Cristina Fernández is passionate. She likes history. She always has. She puts it this way: "Since I was a kid I was always interested in history. Usually, if you like history, you like politics, because they are strongly related. I liked reading about Rosas, the Unitary and the Federal side, but I also loved so much Greek mythology and knew all the names of the Greek Gods — both the Greek version and the Roman. And all the myths and legends. I loved it. That was when I was a small kid. Being already in primary school I loved history all along: Classical Antiquity, The Modern Age, The Renaissance, Napoleon. The only period I never liked was The Middle Ages."

I ask her what she thinks the history books will say about her public performance, but she does not like to think of herself as a woman for monuments. "I have always felt deeply committed to projects and to being part of stories that would leave a mark... always. But the truth is that my dream was never to become President and be one for the history books," she ponders. Then what was her dream when she was just a little girl? "Since childhood I wanted to be a lawyer, she tells me. However, because of an administrative matter, I started studying psychology. I was to become a commercial high school graduate at *Misericordia* School, but I discovered by then that, in order to be admitted to Law School, commercial high school graduates had to sit for around nineteen exams of equivalences. So I started studying psychology, but realised it was not my thing. Luckily, in that year, as fate would have it, Law School admission requirements changed. So I dropped psychology and started Law School, and here I am, a lawyer."

Argentina: Cristina Fernández

Lawyer and President of her country.

Cristina Fernández's political training was marked by different elements, among them, the home confrontation between the ideas of Ofelia Wilhelm, her mother, and Eduardo Fernández, her father. In the words of Cristina: "Dad was, because of his personality, much more reserved than mom, who has a tremendous strength. He was an anti-Peronist. If my father would have had to be a Bedouin in order to be an anti-Peronist, he would have been a Bedouin. The thing is that in that moment, when he was a Radical, Radicalism was very anti-Peronist. He was a Balbinist Radical. He liked the figure of Balbin. He was kind of right-wing, my dad."

Ofelia, on the other hand, is a Peronist, and was by Cristina's side in crucial moments for the movement's ideology — like when Perón returned to Argentina in 1973. On that day of 20 June, momma Ofelia and her eldest daughter were at Ezeiza, and they experienced it. "With gunshots here and there, like everyone else experienced it. There were not many other ways to experience it.

On top of that, we had arrived early. I went with my mother because she wanted to go. I think I could live twenty million years and still remember that day. As soon as we arrived, we heard some gunshots — it was ten in the morning, there were people selling *choripán* sandwiches, and a guy from the vending cart tells me: 'No, it's all right, last night they were firing too.' The best part is that my mother did not want to leave. 'I came to see Perón and I am staying,' she would tell me, and it was already two in the afternoon. We hid behind some trees, but in the end I convinced her and we left," Cristina recounts.

However, Cristina Fernández's fascination with politics can be linked to another family antecedent. When she was a child, she lived with her maternal grandfather, who was also a Peronist. "A Peronist fanatic — adds Cristina — even more than my mom, because he had even hung on to his membership card. He was the one who talked to me about Perón since I was a little girl." To those family influences, Cristina adds the marked climate of those times. During the decade of 1970 it was hard not to take a political position. She tells me that her experience during those years and the discussions that took place in her house both taught her not to believe in extremist things.

The Will to Do

The seventies left a mark on the leaders that grew up during those years

Argentina: Cristina Fernández

— on Cristina Fernández too. I ask her what feeling stands above all the others feelings of those times and she tells me that what is worth recovering is the will to change the state of things. She adds: "The book by Eduardo Anguita and Martín Caparros that reflects the activism of those days, which goes by the name *La Voluntad* (*The Will*), is absolutely accurate regarding what that generation meant. The will, the commitment, the solidarity, thinking in the first person plural and not singular — those are the distinctive trademarks of those years."

Despite her warm memories, the President of Argentina thinks that that agitated decade should not be idealised. Cristina says: "Idealisation makes it more difficult for you to understand reality, which does not mean to accept it. And not understanding the reality makes finding the right path a more difficult task."

I ask her in which respect she thinks some distance is needed regarding those years in the seventies and the changing times that were brewing. She tells me: "After the return of Perón, the effervescence came. But soon Perón was disowned as the leader of the changing process that was taking place in Argentina. I was never in favour of that operation. It was a huge and definitive difference, because it was beyond understanding that the historical process that Perón, Peronism and the people had developed was being ignored."

Several political leaders and students were arrested, for different reasons, during the agitated seventies. I ask her if she was ever arrested too, and she tells me yes, that it was in January 1976, when Isabel Perón was still President. This is her description of that experience:

In 1976 I was arrested, together with Kirchner, a dear friend who had been an activist with us forever, and his wife Mabel. The four of us were arrested on the night of January sixth for alleged infringement of law 19,840, which was the National Security Law. Poor thing Mabel, she had nothing to do with the whole thing. Not only was she neither Peronist nor an activist but she had, all her life, reproached her husband for being Peronist and an activist. She did not understand a thing. She would cry all through the day, and I would try to comfort her. We were at the Third Police Station of Rio Gallegos, which was made for women, because there were no prisons for women. I remember some curious things of that day. There were three regular prisoners. One had tried to poison her husband putting thallium in his mate drink — a small portion every day.

I think she was a sub-officer's wife. Then, another one of them had been arrested after killing her lover in the casitas, the brothels. And another girl that was not arrested, but was rather 'placed' there because her stepfather had attempted to rape her. They had been told that we were two dangerous guerrilla women and they would not get near us under any circumstance. Until some days went by and we started talking through the peephole when the officers would not notice. But, luckily, nothing happened to me. It had a lot to do with who, at the time, was the Federal Intervener of the province, Orlando Parolín, who told the then military leader: "Either you put them at the disposition of the executive power or you let them free, because I do not want political prisoners in my province." They somehow decided to let us free and out we were. It was January and I remember telling Kirchner: "Something terrible is coming."

What was coming was the *coup* of 24 March 1976, the beginning of the bloodiest military dictatorships that Argentina had to endure. The deepest mark it left on Cristina was the feeling of fear. She tells me: "After the dictatorship, I never felt fear again. That pain in your stomach that paralyzes you, that fear, I only felt it during the dictatorship." Cristina confesses to be a person with really low tolerance to physical pain. Her fear, at that time, was the fear of being tortured. Cristina recounts: "I can make a scene because I have an ache. I feel very resistant in other aspects, but I am terrified of physical pain. I remember when I was about to give birth to Máximo that I asked the doctor to give me all the anaesthetics he could so I would not feel pain, and he told me that the baby should not suffer to which I said that neither should the mother."

During the seven years that the dictatorship lasted, a part of what would become the political leaders of the future was suppressed by State terrorism. This is how Cristina sees it: "It is clear that there is a generational hole in the leading classes. Some people were really valuable. I remember Carlos Labolita, a dear friend, a very dear friend, that before disappearing in '76 he gave us — Kirchner and me — a book to each: *Man's* Fate (*The Human Condition*), by André Malraux, and *Megafón, o la Guerra* (*Megaphone, or War*), by Leopoldo Marechal. I still have them." Apart from her personal memories, Cristina argues that individual stories are not the more important ones — the collective ones are. And that one of the problems of postmodernity is that the stories that are written are, above all, individual.

She is Crazy
Ofelia Cédola, a friend of Cristina's from the University of La Plata, gives an overview of the person who is now President of Argentina in those agitated years as a student: "We took several courses together and became close friends. She was one of the few who worked while studying, because most of the others came from the provinces just to study. She was brilliant. Cristina had always been known for being a passionate defender of her ideas. One day, with other students, we were watching her sit for a final exam and we told each other: 'This woman is crazy.' It was just that we could not believe she was presenting her arguments — arguments that were completely opposite to those of the First Holder of the Chair — in such a decisive instance.

The Collective Stories
The current atmosphere in Latin America is very different from that you could feel back in the nineties. The widely held intention is to create collective stories that are not those of the seventies, but new ones. About this, Cristina says: "I think we are living a second independence. The first one was two hundred years ago, when we broke loose of the yoke of colonialism. The second one is the economic independence, which also means more development for our societies and better living conditions for our people."

This issue takes us to the next topic: After having gone through the neoliberal stage and the debate over the seventies, what is, today, the role of the State in Latin America? Cristina Fernández analyses: "This idea that the State does not exist, or, that the State should not exist, that it is a hindrance to the economy was only believed here in Argentina and in Latin America. Not everywhere, though. In Brazil, for example, they did not quite believe it, because Brazilian bourgeoisie, the business sector, has a much stronger sense of belonging."

The new generation of Latin American political leaders has a lot to do, also, with a different view regarding the region's unity — a unity that is built from diversity. Cristina thinks: "Great effort is needed, obviously, because there are interests and differences. But I think it is really worth the effort. The important thing is to start finding procedures, instruments and mechanisms to process those differences so that we can continue to work and so that we can prevent — above everything else — conflicts that would end up serving extra-regional interests. That is clear for all of us, for everyone, and I think it has been evident, in the meetings we have had, how this is working. Besides the verbal excesses each of us may have, the styles and manners, there is a clear understanding of the limits — limits that cannot be exceeded, because that would put the regional issue in danger.

Latin American union is another topic that makes Cristina's arguments become firm, heart felt, compelling. She continues: "I think that what Latin America needs is not a message. I think that what it needs are deeds and policies from those of us who have governmental responsibilities. We all have the need to know that the region is destined to play a leading role in the twenty first century, but only if we can process our differences, and mainly accept them in the framework of a mutual, collective construction. Our destiny is common and collective. Because history shows that every time we have had confrontation, divisions, separations, it has been really bad for us. It is impossible to pretend we are all the same because we are indeed different. But it has not been the case, never before, that each of us resembles their societies so much."

There is another collective story that takes us again to the experiences of past decades, and comes back to the present in the form of a bridge. That story is the one that has to do with the *Guerra de las Malvinas* (Falklands War). Cristina Fernández defines herself as a "very Malvinist" person, and shares her vision on the war and its consequences: "When you take a look at the families of the combatants, you see that the great majority of them are very poor families. It is always the case that the ones who die for the country are the poorer, the ones that have the least. And in the wars for the independence it was exactly like that. The people have always had a sense of pride and belonging to the homeland — something that is not often the case when it comes to the wealthier classes."

From this point of view, the debate over the *Guerra de Malvinas* leads to an unsettled issue in the everyday life of the millions of inhabitants of Latin America: its great inequality. On this topic, Cristina reflects: "Being the Argentine President, one of my greatest goals is for all of us to live in a fairer country. We still have an unfair, inequitable country — not only in terms of income distribution, but also regarding recognition. I think it is a country that does not treat everyone the same way. If you live in the centres of the country and, besides, you have blue eyes and blonde hair, you have more opportunities than someone who lives in the Northern provinces, comes from a *Colla* community and has darker skin. I think justice is not only in the economic aspect, but also in the social recognition and, above all other things, in treating everyone with respect and equality."

The Future

Cristina Fernández would not like national heroes to last only as marble figures, and would not like to see herself become that. But there are some features of her administration that she would like for history books of the future to remember. She lists them like this: "First, I would like to be remembered for the changes I made, and because I deepened the processes that needed to be deepened. One of the most important things, in my opinion, is to have pushed forward the *Ley Servicios de Medios Audiovisuales* (Audio-visual Media Law). Since the year 1983, since the advent of democracy, it had not been possible to make that change. It was a debate that spread all over the country. There is also the issue of the workers funds management, and what is and will continue to be the struggle for the redistribution of income."

Other topics come up. Cristina Fernández looks full of pride at having managed, during her administration, to pay up the International Monetary Fund and having started the end of Argentina's default. To that, she adds the Supreme Court of Justice's reform that put an end to what was known as the "automatic majority" that was imposed during Carlos Menem's presidencies during the nineties. "It was a very important act of institutional quality, and I must acknowledge the part played by the Parliament in that time, because it echoed a demand made by society," Cristina says.

The overview of her actions as President, leads her to make some reflections about the role that politics have to play in current societies: "Politics have to change things. If I thought that there was nothing to change, it would be because I think everything is all right. And if I think that everything is all right, then I would stay at home and not go into politics. I think politics is a deep nonconformity with the world around you — a world that you have to make better and change from your perspective, from your view, which is arguable, is debatable, but that, if you live in a democracy and you try to do it in a democratic manner, it is absolutely valid and respectable."

Before saying her goodbyes, Cristina says that she would not like her figure to be reduced, many years from now, to a picture in a frame. And she adds: "You have to resist that temptation of becoming your own historian. I think you have to let history flow and do what you have to do responsibly, and at the right time. And then, history will tell." Yes, history will tell.

BOLIVIA: EVO MORALES
TO TAKE DOWN THE INDIAN

Juan Evo Morales Ayma was born on 6 October 1959, in a community called Isallavi, in the Orinoca District, really close to the lake Poopó de Oruro. His first trade union post was when he was named Sports Secretary at the Sindicato de Colonizadores de Chapare in 1983. He has been Executive Secretary of the Tropic of Cochabamba Federation since 1988, and he has been President of the Committee for the Coordination of the Six Federations of the Tropic of Cochabamba since 1996. He was elected as National Deputy for the circumscription 27, Chapare, in 1997. In January 2006 he was elected President of Bolivia and was re-elected in December 2009 and again in 2014. His term will end in 2020. Since 2007, several Latin American social institutions have proposed him for the Nobel Peace Prize for his contributions in defence of Mother Earth. The request was made official by the Bolivian Legislature in April 2010.

"We have to take down the *Indian*". The Latin American President, who comes from the continent's native communities, has heard this expression many times since 22 January 2006. On that day, the *Indian* at hand, Evo Morales, became President of Bolivia. The *Indian* that, according to the Bolivian oligarchic sectors, has to be taken down.

Evo Morales knows he has a great responsibility. You can tell it by the way he speaks, breathes and moves his hands to express himself. If he is not a good president, then never again will someone from the native communities rise to power — in Bolivia or anywhere else in Latin America. "So I have this idea in my mind: I have to try and be the best President," he tells me.

Evo comes from an Aymara family, and thus, there are three expressions he cannot forget: *ama sua, ama quella* and *ama hulla*. They mean, respectively, do not be a thief, do not be lazy, and do not be a liar, and they are ancestral mandates that every Aymara must honour. For Evo, these features are the ones that led him to being President of Bolivia — even though he himself does not feel like a president. Evo says: "Now I am kind of getting used to it, but I do not feel like a president. The greetings, the protocol, the *aides-de-camp*, are all things I do not understand. I feel as if I have lost my privacy. I like it better when I am having conversations with mates, the people of the town, even if it can bring trouble. Really, I do not feel like a president."

In some other sense, his critics do not feel he is Bolivia's political leader. "I did not know that there were lodges in my country," Evo tells me, and I can see in him a certain air of surprise. "They are oligarchic groups that went: 'Poor little Indian, let him be president for two weeks or three, then he will leave, we will make him leave, he will not be able to govern.' One year passed, and in a 2007 report they said: 'This Indian is staying for a long time, something must be done.' That year went by, and by the end they said: 'How do we take down the Indian? Let's take him down with inflation, with abrupt swings in the economy'. They all think only about taking down the Indian. I want to tell to the opposing sector, that maybe by some chance you may be able to take down the Indian, but you will never take down the people."

Sitting down in front of Evo Morales is like having a conversation with five hundred years of injustice y oblivion to the communities that own the lands of the Americas. It is like being able to see them smile, now that they can witness this historical process.

Evito and the Dreams

Evo is now just a child that sleeps, and while he does, he dreams he walks among snakes and he does not know where to set down his feet. He weeps; he wakes up crying and tells his mother: "Mom, I dreamt of the viper." She replies: "Evito, you are going to have a lot of money." Full of emotion, Evo Morales tells his story, and suddenly his mother, his dreams and his crying are present in the office we are having our conversation. "I do not have much money, but I have enough to live," adds Evo, and recounts another dream: "I was about fourteen or fifteen, and I dreamt I was flying, and a cloud came over.

And I thought: 'If I get into the cloud... How will I see? What will I see?' And I got scared, and again I cried. And I told my father that I had dreamt that I was flying and that I had woken up crying. 'You will do well in the future, Evito; you have to respect the elder and the young in order to be respected in life'. I think my dreams, often in my life, serve me as a guide."

These anecdotes show us that, for Evo, childhood is a territory to be explored once and again, a refuge where to search for teachings and life values. Evo continues: "I think the best legacy my family has left me is honesty. When I was a child, they would always talk about honesty, transparency... about being sincere. My father would tell me that if I was lacking something I had to borrow it, or to ask for it as a gift, but never steal, never lie. It is a basic principle." Evito was a smiling, happy boy who learnt lessons from his father Dionisio and his mother María while playing around all the time. Evo recounts that his father would tell him that he looked like a "happy dummy". To make it more graphic, he tells a story: "As a child, you are always happy. Most probably, my parents must have been experiencing economic difficulties, and I would whistle and sing and chase the sheep and the llamas. Once, I remember my father asking me to walk the pig and I rode it instead of walking it. The pig would throw me to the ground and I would get back up only to be thrown again. And then, my uncles tell me, I spent all day embracing the pig, and my most vivid memory is riding that pig, happy, getting home. That is why my father called me a happy dummy. I ran around, happy. I did not have much trouble as a kid."

I tell him that there is something that makes us, Argentines, very proud and it is that he spent a part of his childhood in Calilegua, in the Province of Jujuy. Evo takes some minutes to recall that experience:

There were some neighbours, some uncles that would constantly go to the Argentine sugar harvest, where they were recruiting workers. One time, it was my dad who decided to go to the harvest. I was about five or six years old and went with him, along with my sister. We spent some time at Villazón and from there we crossed to La Quiaca. Several days went by as we waited for the train to come, until finally we were able to take it and we got to Argentina. And then we stayed at a camping site in Calilegua. We did not have any food; all there was around was sugar, and some noodles that were toasted. There were some oranges that to me were a treat. After some time living there, came the time for me to go to school — it was compulsory for kids to do so. I was really scared because I did not really know any Spanish. They would call the roll — they would say "Evo Morales" — and I would not say anything, because I did not know how to reply. And so, I would stay in the back, sitting. Then we changed camping site, harvest was over, and I would not go to school any longer because it was too far away. I then learned to swim in the river. What I remember the most, is that, as a result of this trip to Argentina, we were able, for the first time, to buy a cot — a portable bed. Before that, we all slept on the ground. And this little cot we brought back with us is part of our history, and it is still there — the first bed that the Morales family ever knew. Thanks to the harvest and to our trip to Argentina.

Education is a main topic for the Bolivian President, and has troubled him since his childhood. When Evo was a child, his mother told him about an uncle that had been the first person from Orinoca District who could read and write. And Evo asked: 'How did he learn to read and write?' It was not a silly question. There could be no school in the Orinoca District. It was completely forbidden for indigenous people to study. That is why there was a school that worked — in the shadows — in a hut. Evo tells me that when he first had the chance to read some of the supporters of the indigenous movement, like Fausto Reinaga, he was surprised to discover that the first Quechua people that learnt to read and write were punished — their hands were cut off or their eyes removed.

I ask him if it is possible, nowadays, to preserve the native languages through school. "It is another debate," he tells me. "Yes, as long as there is a university in native languages. When, at one time, the intention was to implement the native languages in schools, it was at first accepted, but then the fathers of families protested. I remember when I ran the Six Federations meetings and the Tropic of Cochabamba Federation and the parents would say: 'We agree that they should learn in Aymara and in Quechua, but it is important too, that they learn very good Spanish and another foreign language.' I would ask then why Spanish and why English or French or German, and they would tell me: 'Because the texts are in those languages. There is no university in Aymara or in Quechua. And when they refuse to teach Spanish in schools, they want our children to pay the price, they do not want our children going to the university.' And they were right."

Evo's House

A settler of Orinoca District, in Oruro, showed us the house where Evo lived during his childhood. It is an adobe house, as simple as it gets, and one could say, using a common place, that it is in the middle of nowhere. Actually, it is in the middle of the countryside, and confirms the President's origins, that some foreign visitors still cannot believe. According to the same settler, tourists think Evo must surely have lived in a three-storey building as a child. But no — Evo is a man of the country, and in the country there are no tower buildings.

The other big matter that marked Evo Morales since childhood — and is still present in the President's mind — is nutrition. According to Evo, his father did not worry about their children's clothes being worn out — it should be used until it is no longer functional. "We can have trouble with our clothes, but never with our stomachs," Dionisio would say. There were times that there was nothing but corn — corn for breakfast, lunch and dinner. There were other times when meat would appear, and we would eat sheep or llama. And whatever works that were done, they were done in order to feed the family. "Eating comes first," Evo's father would say; and that voice repeats itself like an echo in Evito's vision — that kid that would ride a pig around with a smile on his face — now that he runs the destiny of an entire country.

The Union Leader

"I am not, actually, a native authority, because all my training is that of a union leader." Evo's remark has to do with his double rise to power in 2006: on the one hand, as President of Bolivia, and on the other, as the top indigenous authority. Evo says that his parents actually were native authorities, and to see them at work helped him train himself as a leader. Evo recounts: "I have seen from up close how they handled things, how they walked and how they mobilised for social vindication. The union aspect is really different."

In 1980, an extensive and severe draught forced the Morales Ayma family to relocate from the Orinoca region to Chapare, in Cochabamba. There, Evo Morales — by then twenty one years old — began working in the coca fields, and soon discovered the adverse living conditions that came with the job. It was one of the triggers for his involvement in trade union activity. The other event that forever marked the life of the young Evo Morales was the assassination of a coca worker at Senda Bayer, Chipiriri region, in 1981. On that occasion, a group of military of the de facto government of Luis García Meza Tejada beat up a worker because he would not declare himself guilty of trafficking drugs. Then, they poured fuel on him. On that day, Evo promised himself to fight for human rights and for the free cultivation of coca.

In 1983, Morales was elected Sport Secretary of the *Colonizadores de Chapare* Trade Union, which gathers representatives from over ten native towns from the high lands of the Andes in search for better living conditions. Since then, he has been appointed General Secretary of his trade union, Executive Secretary of the Tropic Federation, and President of the Committee for the Coordination of the Six Federations of the Tropic of Cochabamba. Evo's prestige as a trade unionist is the great motor behind his journey to the political arena. He explains: "When I was 27 I got the possibility to run the Federation, and I said to myself that if I did not meet the expectations as a trade union leader, never again would the new generations, the youth, be able to run the Tropic Federation." It is, clearly, what Evo thinks about his current administration.

What was it like to be a renowned trade unionist back then? The President of Bolivia says: "There was no place for any type of fun, because the important thing was to defend yourself as a union leader. I remember very clearly how I would go up into the wilderness carrying my television, my videos and an electric generator. We would then watch recordings of the struggles in Ecuador, in Peru and in many countries until eleven in the night. Then we would stop to drink some beer until one or two in the morning, and then we would continue working."

Evo Morales also recounts that, when he was a union leader, presidents, ministers and leaders of the Catholic Church would approach him to try and stop his activity. "They would offer me bribes, both directly and indirectly, and they even offered me a scholarship for the university."

Once, the President of Bolivia said that his only full time activity, his true passion was — and still is — the protection of the leaf of coca, of the land and of the territory. However, that unionist who loves the countryside had to mutate and take a step forward to change the history of his country: Evo Morales became a political leader.

Evo Makes Politics

Bolivian history seemed to set a course that was difficult to change. The country workers were used, left and right, as a springboard for political careers to take off. But once many of those politicians made it to the National Parliament, the indigenous people's cause was left behind. The solution, then, was for a trade union leader, defender of the indigenous people's rights, to get to Parliament.

In 1995, the farmers' and indigenous people's organisations founded the Political Instrument for the Sovereignty of the Peoples (Spanish: IPSP), that had a great goal: to take on the local and national power. The National Electoral Court denied the IPSP their initials and their legal capacities, and thus the new group approached the elections as Movement for Socialism (Spanish: MAS). In 1997, Evo Morales was already Deputy and his political career was just beginning. How did he feel those early moments? In the voice of Evo: "At Chapare, I would sometimes go as base delegate to some meetings, negotiations. And there were Federation leaders who, whenever some leader would present some serious proposal or structural change, would say: 'No, no. You are making politics. Your politics is with the axe and machete, with work.' We could not bring up programmatic or ideological proposals."

Evo recounts that those circumstances ended up with the neoliberal parties going to the meetings to offer bribes to get votes. The result was that the farmers would end up voting against their own interests, and the neoliberal parties would win the elections. Morales explains: "It happened in 1995, for example. Víctor Paz Estensoro won the elections, the Nationalist Revolutionary Movement (Spanish: MNR) won in the country, and in the mining centres, picture it, Hugo Banzer Suárez, the dictator, won. Of course, none of them won with the fifty per cent plus one, but they banded together in the National Congress. Thus, they were free to impose programmes against the farmer's movement, against the popular movement, against the worker's and mining movement. And I reflected: How did they — with our votes — impose policies against us?"

For Evo Morales, the key is to build a political movement that gives room to moving forward, to debates and discussions. "Because the vote is important," Evo says, "I really believe in the consciousness of the people." After that, everything hastened. In 2002, MAS got over half a million votes and was allowed to put thirty six members in congress. Since 2004, MAS is the main political force of the country.

Evo tells me that in 2002 his party was not ready to govern yet. Even though he thinks the voting was irregular and repeats: "They have stolen my election," he also admits it was not the time for his arrival at power. Evo says: "I was candidate for the Presidency for the first time in 2002. At that time, we only had a tender, like any trade union organisation, where it was stated, in general: "I want this, this and this." But there was no programme. And even so, we got in second place. Five legally constituted parties, recognised by the National Electoral Court, beat us by one per cent. And I got scared. Because if we had made an alliance with other parties in order to win, then we would have let the people down and we would not have governed well. I feel that the empire, the United States' ambassador, was not clever enough. If I had been the US ambassador, instead of gathering all the right wing parties to stop me from becoming President, I would have taken 'that lefty' who had only 27 out of 130 congressmen, and name him President and he would not have been able to govern. If that had happened, then we would have lasted less than a year. And it would have been a complete failure." But in that distant 2002, the one who finally became President was Gonzalo Sánchez de Lozada.

In 2010, Evo Morales had already started his second presidential term. Why was it necessary to have more than one term in order to push forward effective policies? Evo answers: "More time is needed to consolidate the changes, the processes. Within five years you cannot promise any kind of structural, social and cultural change. That was very important in the trade union dispute, because if I had not been supported for so many years, I would have never become President of Bolivia."

Father Government

Evo Morales knows he is not alone as he walks this path. The political moment that Latin America is going through is very different now from what it was ten years ago when we could still hear neoliberalism's death rattle. Evo says: "I think what Latin America is experiencing is fascinating. It is a great rebellion of the people against the empire, against multinational corporations, against the plundering of our natural resources. It is the rebellion for social justice."

I ask him if he thinks that the process that is taking place in Bolivia is related to what is going on in the rest of the continent, and he gives me a surprising answer: "I think each region, each country, is different, but we complement each other and what drives our commitment is finding a way to solve the social problems, especially regarding basic services, in terms of energy, water and communication. This complementary quality between presidents, between governments, is going to play a big role in consolidating these processes in Latin America."

Many times I have read columns in liberal media that expressed concern about the spread of "populist governments" in Latin America. They would talk about semi-dictatorships when referring to Morales or Chávez, accusing these governments of trying to impose one single way of looking at reality. And now Evo says that the great value of these leaders of the region is that they are different from each other. And he continues: "Latin America's great advantage is unity with great respect for diversity. It is what we always fight for: unity, but respect for diversity — beginning with their presidents, who are so diverse.

Bolivia: Evo Morales

Five O'Clock in the Morning

The taxi driver who is taking us to our meeting with Evo Morales is proud of the President of his country. And he recounts: "I work from as early as five in the morning, and I always see my President. I finish around eleven or midnight, and the light in his office is still lit. Then I realise that all that time he has been working." The taxi driver adds a reflection on the current political process: "Our President is trying very hard. He is carrying out a peaceful revolution. One of them comes from workers' trade union struggles, one from farmers' trade union struggles; there are intellectuals, there are women, there are military, economists. Now there is even a priest, incidentally."

A central variable in this conception of "Patria Grande" (Great Homeland) is the making up of UNASUR, the Union of South American Nations. Evo says: "UNASUR serves as an organism that leads the way for Latin America regarding our own internal problems, without the boss. There is no longer an empire that can subdue us. UNASUR is there to free us from the empire."

When Evo speaks about politics, he does so with the same spontaneity that he has when he speaks about the Aymaran traditions, or his life in the country, or football. And always with a smile on his face.

I tell him that, in that political scene, inequality is still a problem in the region — because Latin America is not the poorest continent, but it is the one with most inequality. The inevitable question arises: What is the best tool to fight inequality in Latin America? Evo says that that tool is being used in Bolivia and gives some concrete examples: "We have decided to hand out credits with zero per cent interest for four very important products: wheat, rice, corn and soybeans. Those small entrepreneurs, those micro-entrepreneurs, they already have funds to start and they are making progress. Before that, banks would hand out credits but with an interest of 36 per cent annually."

And then, the key comes up — the most precise definition on how to articulate policies that would lead to lowering inequality. "I call it Father Government," Evo stresses. State involvement is paramount. Of course, during the eighties we were told that, regarding corruption, regarding unemployment, private enterprises were the social solution. But, as we have seen, unemployment rose when, within the context of neoliberalism, they tried to eliminate the State."

Bolivia's President is passionate about explaining the benefits of a strong government. Father Government. He says that the State is central to production and not just to policy and regulatory framework. He talks about Yacimientos Petrolíferos Fiscales Bolivianos (YPFB) — that state-owned company created in 1936 to explore, produce, distil and sell oil and its by-products. Evo says there is no bigger company in Bolivia than YPFB, and he is proud, because as he speaks he remembers the company's partial privatisation in 1997 during the Gonzalo Sánchez de Lozada's government, and how it was nationalised in 2006. "YPFB belongs completely to the State, to the people," Evo reflects.

With regards to the environmental issue, Bolivia's President is convinced that Latin America is the world's natural resources reservoir, but he risks a criticism of the environmentalists: "The Europeans, with the pretext that they are protecting the environment, do not want Latin America to have energy. They do not want us setting up thermoelectric, hydroelectric or geothermic plants. All in the name of protecting the environment, to save their lives, but they are the ones who end up destroying it. It is important to protect the environment, but it is also important to gather energy for the people. I am a defender of the environment, but let us not be fooled. There are non-governmental foundations and organisations that confuse our people. Those differences need to be discussed."

The Bolivian President's political idea is then a mixture of environmental protection, national sovereignty and the search for South American cooperation against the interests of the world's powers. In the voice of Evo: "We need to fight for the protection of the natural resources; the poor and exploited people rights, the thousands workers and unemployed ones; the refunding of our motherland and the protection of life itself. Instead of being subdued by empire, let us be subdued by the people. The people will be the best judge for us presidents, vice presidents, and prefects"

The Aftermath

I ask Evo how he would like to be remembered as President of Bolivia. Evo does not know exactly how he wants to go down in history, simply because he never thought he would do so. I ask him again: What would you like your children to say about you? And then he says: "Each family, not only Evo Morales', would always like to serve, and even more if we have political responsibilities." His eyes glow. "I would like to be remembered by the people as so many other leaders... Tupac Catari, Father Luis Espinal, Che Guevara." The family tree is not bad: an Aymara that fought against the colony in Alto Peru in the eighteenth century; a priest that came from Spain to fight for human rights; a revolutionary Argentinian; and the first Latin American leader to come from native descent.

What comes next for this leader of indigenous descent? What is a President like after being President? "When my administration is over, I will find a partner and go to Chapare," says Evo with simplicity, and now it becomes clear what he wants, and his eyes are filled with that tropical paradise where he will be able to cultivate coca peacefully, without protocol, without noises, without any one to greet by obligation.

BRAZIL: "LULA" DA SILVA
THE WORKER

Luiz Inácio da Silva was born on 7 October 1945, in the city of Garanhuns, in the urban peripheries of the state of Pernambuco. He is married and has five children. He got his first job at the age of twelve at a dry cleaner's and before he came of age he passed the course of the National Service for Industrial Training (Portuguese: SENAI) and became a lathe operator. In 1969, he was elected to the Secretariat of the Metal Workers Union of São Bernardo do Campo. In 1972 he became First Secretary. In 1975 he became President of the Union, and was re-elected after three years. On 10 February 1980, he founded the PT, Partido dos Trabalhadores — Workers' Party. In August 1983, he was involved in the creation of CUT, Central Unica dos Trabalhadores — Workers' Central Office. In 1986, he was elected Federal Deputy for the Constituent Assembly. He was a Presidential candidate in 1989, 1994 and 1998 and was defeated each time. In 2002, he won the Presidential elections with almost 53 million votes, a record number up to that moment in the history of the country. He was re-elected in 2006, and took office again on 1 January 2007. His administration ended in December 2010.

"I did not like politics."

It is a phrase uttered by the leader who governed Brazil from 1 January 2003. How can it be possible that a President who was in office for eight years did not like politics? Lula da Silva explains: "Up to 1978 my world was all about the union movement, the struggle of the worker. But two years later I was founding a political party, choosing a candidate for governor, and then I turned to President of the Republic."

Lula is the first union leader of Latin America ever to have got to the Presidency of his country. Does his past as a worker represent any kind of special responsibility for him? Lula says: "Yes, my responsibility is higher than that of an upper-middle class president, or a businessman president, or an intellectual president. Why? Because my election overcame many preconceptions. Later, my administration also had to face many preconceptions, and one has to be there every day to prove himself capable. I insist, every day. I always say that when an upper class President loses an election or ends his administration, they spend a year in New York, in London, two years in Paris. Not me. When I am through, I am going back to São Bernardo do Campo. That is to say, I go back to six hundred metres from the union that raised me. That is why I have to do things right. Every single day I wake up with the obligation to do things right, because if I fail the people, it could take us another thirty or forty years to get our heads back up. I think that my responsibility, as well as that of Evo Morales in Bolivia, is far greater than that of those who belong to a social class that rules countries more often than not."

Lula da Silva knows that his arrival in office gives hope to the working classes, because they can see themselves reflected in him. He expands on the thought: "I think that inspiring the thought in the minds of the most humble that they can get to a good place, that they can be winners, is a wonderful thing. And I say this in many talks with the social movement. Even though you might have problems in your life, do not feel discouraged. We have to show determination, we have to fight. I always say to the young people: 'When you no longer trust any politician, get into politics!' Because, maybe, the perfect politician that this young man needs is himself — and not some elected other. It is all in the spirit of saying to the young: 'If you want to win, go where you never imagined you would go.' Every day we need to fight for something, every day we must build something, even in adversity. I lost three elections. I could have given up, but I made it because I was persistent. Every time I lost an election, I would come home and my wife would tell me: 'It is enough, Lula; you have already lost one election, you have already lost three.' But I would lose an election in November and in January I would already be travelling throughout Brazil. Why? To boost the morale of my troops."

I ask Lula if there has been any referent in his family that instructed him in the ways of overcoming adversity. To answer me, the President tells a long story, heartfelt and precise, that is worth reproducing:

I think that what I am about to say applies to Argentina, Venezuela, Brazil, Paraguay. It applies to all countries. We have a problem in Latin America. In the past thirty years there has been a process of family structure disintegration. Misery — that leads to drinking, that leads to unemployment, that leads to the break-up of marriages, that leads to domestic violence — made children lose their referents. That is a very serious problem we are experiencing nowadays, especially in the great capitals' peripheral neighbourhoods. But I thank God because, despite everything, my mother was able to raise eight children in a completely adverse situation. My mother never stopped being the referent. For example, until I was eighteen, I received my salary in the factory and I handed it to my mother in the same way I received it: a closed envelope. The salary was not mine, it was hers. And that woman, who was illiterate, managed to raise a family of eight brothers and sisters in total and absolute harmony. We never fought each other. Many times we had differences, naturally, because we were so many people in one house, because we were thirteen people living in one room — but that was all. My mother separated from my father, she left home and without a job she took on the adventure of travelling to São Paulo. There, we lived in the backroom of a bar, and shared the only toilet — not just between us, but also with the customers. So, if there is a marked figure in the family structure — may be the father or the mother — that is balanced, then the possibilities of building an honourable family are total and absolute. My mother raised eight children in great misery, and none of them turned into a thief, none of them became a crook. I think there are millions of mothers in Latin America that take care of their children, even in adversity — women with courage. Because there are woman that submit to their husbands because they are unemployed and they depend on their husband's salary. In Brazil, in Argentina, anywhere in Latin America, a mother knows her responsibilities left and right, and is far more competent than any man to run a family. And mine is that example; that is why she is my referent.

Lula's parents died thirty years ago, but in that time, he could not say goodbye to them. Both died during times when their child was being held prisoner for participating in different strikes. First of all, the President of Brazil talks about the circumstances of his father's death, and gives us a profile of his personality: "My father died in 1978. I was being held prisoner at the time for protesting against Ernesto Geisel's dictatorship. My father had twenty one children, because he had other women, and still, he died a homeless man. None of his children were close to him. He was a hard man, a very bad man. He was not the father that children ought to have. When I received a letter with the news, he had been dead for thirteen days. Today I have forgiven him, but he was not a good father."

In April 1980, Lula da Silva led a strike that lasted forty one days and was comprised of 270 thousand workers from São Paulo. Because of that strike, he was imprisoned for a month. And during that time his mother died. He recounts: "My mother did not know I was in jail because my brothers and I managed to keep her away from the television so she would not find out. She was sick. Then, when it was time for the funeral, they let me go and two delegates took me to the cemetery. The funny thing is that after the funeral was over, the fellow workers did not want to let me go back to prison, they would not let me go into the police car. They started throwing stones and bricks at the car. Right then I had to convince them to let me go back to prison, because there were still thirteen fellow workers there."

Lula feels moved when he talks about his mother, and that emotion is transmitted in every word he says, in every gesture he makes. I ask him if there is any time during his working hours as President when he imagines what his mother would say if she could see him now that he is President. Lula says: "No, I cannot imagine. In 1961, when I was a student at SENAI, the National Service for Industrial Training, it was glorious for her, because I was going to have the right to learn a profession. Being the youngest, I was the first of my brothers to have a profession. I imagine that if my mother would be alive to see her youngest child as President of the Republic, to her, it would be the best. But, as I believe in other lives, I think she is already watching this."

Do you appeal to the memory of your mother whenever you, as President of Brazil, have any doubt regarding a decision making situation? He answers: "No, no. I do not demand that of her. See, I find no difficulties in making a decision — although I always need a second, third or fourth opinion. If I can summon a social movement to speak, I summon it, because the more people you listen to, the easier to make the decision becomes. Thus, I think my mother is in every step I take. Even though I do not ask her for help, she is pushing me through my decisions at all times."

Fate in his Hands
The President of Brazil has the chance to change the living conditions of all his countrymen. Not just because he is the leader of his country, but also because he has experience in having his fate, and the fate of others, in his hands. There is no other leader in the region that has had a manual industrial work experience. When he was eighteen he started working as a lathe operator. What was that experience like? He recounts: "It was real manual labour. There were no automatic lathes like there are today, or a programmed lathe in which you set a program and the pieces

come out ready. In those times, everything had to be done manually. It was almost a craftwork. It was something beautiful and gratifying. Besides, that profession allowed me to go from earning minimum wage to earning ten minimum wages. My life changed substantially; because as a lathe operator I could afford a car, take my wife out to dinner twice a month and made more money than a doctor. It is because of my training as a lathe operator that I am here today. If it was not for that, I do not know what would have been of me and my future. That is the truth. If I had stayed in the northeast, I would have been dead already — like many of my relatives that died because of their drinking, of cirrhosis; because there is nothing they can do, they do not have the opportunity to work. I thank God that my mother decided to come to São Paulo."

The moving took place when Lula was seven years old. The trip lasted thirteen days. The Brazilian leader recounts it like this: "The truck that took us there had no seats. There were chunks of wood lying around where you would sit without any kind of support for your back. There was nothing to hold on to either. In the middle of the trip I saw a Shell truck that was carrying oil. Since then, my dream had been to become a truck driver — but not any truck driver; *that* truck driver."

Did that kid have any other dream? He says: "I confess I did not dream of becoming President, I never dreamt of being a politician. My dream was a very small one. I had to dream about what we were going to have for breakfast, and after breakfast I had to dream about what we would have for lunch, and after lunch I had to dream about what we were going to have for dinner — it was survival law."

Lula da Silva did not dream of becoming President, but he attempted it four times. He lost three consecutive elections, and the fourth one was a charm. He already told me that after losing one of those elections, he had to recover quickly so as not to discourage his fellow workers. But, was he ready to win in those early presentations? He recounts: "In 1989, in my first defeat against Fernando Collor de Mello, I had the whole election in my hands; I came so close I could embrace victory. But we made a mistake that came from inexperience. For example, when the day of the final debate came, I had not slept in over thirty six hours — and you know, when you do not sleep well enough your head does not function correctly. I went through with it — even though I should have not. I lost the debate and I lost the elections, but, do you want to know what I think today? I think God's hand was there, because we should not have won those elections. We were too radical, and if I had won, with the discourse we had at the time, I think we would not have governed for more than eight months. When I won in 2002, we had already matured. At that moment we were truly able to govern the country."

With the Family

José Ferreira da Silva, Lula's brother, takes us to a bar where his daughter works. She asks about Lula. Frei Chico — that is what they call him — answers: "Lula is fine. He is in the mad world. That thing is slavery, but he likes it." Later, already seated, he tells us about his brother: "Lula has no life. His life, over the last forty years, has been dedicated to the cause". Manuel Ferreira de Melo, Lula's cousin, remembers the current Brazilian President's mother: "She never called him Lula. She would just call him Luiz. Every time he went around on some mischief — because he was quite a thing, that boy — she would tell him: 'Luiz come right here!'" And Manuel tells us a story that describes his cousin: "You may think: 'I am a simple truck driver, my President cousin will not remember me.' But he did, and sent me an invitation to the day of his inauguration. Along came the invitation and an airplane ticket for me to go wearing a suit." Another of Lula's cousins, Gilberto Ferreira de Melo, reflects: "To this date, Lula has given me nothing, but he has given to the Brazilian people. We do not need his help. Of this soil I live, and envy no one in this world."

Now, Luiz Inácio Lula da Silva has finished his second term as President of Brazil. Overcoming adversities has been central in his education, both political and personal. How did he manage to turn all that unpleasantness to his favour? Did he have any particular characteristic that helped him become President? Lula gives his opinion: "I consider myself to be a very lucky man in life. There must be some greater thing that helped me get to where I am, and in the way I did. If it is not sheer magic, and it is not because of my intelligence, it is because there is something greater that goes on in life, and one can only believe it or not. I do. I went through a lot of hardship — a lot. So I had all the opportunities in the world to become a bitter man, but I am not one. I never won any prize in my life. It was only when I was seventeen that I bought myself a rubber ball. Then, as a second present to myself, I bought an old bicycle that would be constantly losing its chain. In 1965 there was a big economic crisis, and I became unemployed for more than one year and a half. Then my mother would see that four of her children were unemployed, and there was nothing to eat — yet, I never saw her complain about the lack of food. I think that those things formed my belief in complaining less. If you have nothing, instead of complaining, you have to fight for the things you want, you have to search."

Lula searched and searched, and in 1966 he joined the union life. He worked for an important metal company, Industrias Villares, which was established in the zone of São Bernardo do Campo, one of the municipalities of the metropolitan area of São Paulo. And the key in his change of direction was the influence of his brother José Ferreira da Silva, best known as Frei Chico. Which role did Frei Chico play in Lula's decision? The President of Brazil tells us: "He was a member of the Communist Party, but nobody knew, because it was all clandestine. And in 1972 the opportunity came for him to become Director of the metal union, but he could not take it, because of his condition as clandestine member of the Communist Party. Besides, there already was a director in the factory where he was working. So he said to the managers: 'Why don't you call my brother Lula who is working at Villares?' And they called me. I was scared, because in those times, the military regime was really hard here. There was persecution of the communists, of the fellow workers that were in the armed struggle. My entrance to the union world was thanks to my brother."

Lula mentions Frei Chico as the most politicised of his brothers. He recounts that they used to argue a lot because his brother would ask him to go to secret meetings, but Lula did not want to meet that way. Lula said about those times: "I will not go to any clandestine meeting! Because what you say in those clandestine meetings I say it in the doorsteps of the factory." And so Frei Chico would get nervous and worried. "We would give speeches that many intellectually trained people would not because they were afraid," Lula says. In 1975, Frei Chico was captured and tortured by the military dictatorship regime. When he got out, his brother Lula would say to him: "Why don't you seek vengeance on the man that tortured you? You could find the man that tortured you and beat him up." But Frei Chico would only say: "No. It is over."

After his brother's first push, Lula made his own way as a union man. He was elected President of the Metal Union in that same year of 1975. He won with 92 per cent of the votes and was suddenly representing a hundred thousand workers. He was re-elected in 1978, and his actions deeply changed the Brazilian union movement. After ten years without a strike, a hundred and seventy five thousand metal workers went on full strike in Sao Paulo.

How did that worker's leader come to politics when it was clear that it did not call his attention? What was it like to move from union struggle to national power dispute? The consequences of the strikes were key to this. Lula recounts: "I think there is an evolution in every human political conscience. In 1978 I was President of the Metal Union, and suddenly I saw that I needed to get into politics to do the things I thought the other presidents should be doing. In that same year, here in Brazil, we had a Minister of Labour who wrote a law that forbade strikes by essential categories such as bankers, gas station workers or teachers. I rebelled against that law and came to Brasilia to the Deputies Chamber to speak to them and tell them that they could not pass that law. It was in that moment that I realised that workers had no representation whatsoever in the National Congress. I went back to Sao Paulo thinking: 'How can I be hoping for laws that would benefit the working class if we do not have any worker in the National Congress?' And right there, on 5 July 1978, the day my son was born, it was the first time I said that a party of workers needed to be created in order to give power to the people in this country. It took twenty four years for the *Partido dos Trabalhadores* (Workers' Party) to win a Presidential Election. The fact is that we managed to organise a party, we organised our union central and we reached government."

The American Giant

In 2010, Lula was the President of two hundred million people. Brazil is the fifth most populated country in the world, and without a doubt the biggest reference Latin America has towards the world. It has the biggest territory, it is the most industrialised, and it has the strongest economy. The success of the region depends, in real terms, on the success Brazil has. How do you manage the leadership Brazil has over the other countries in Latin America? Lula thinks: "Actually, I do not like to talk about leadership. Each country has its own sovereignty. It is only possible to be a leader if you are elected, and thus, I cannot say I was the leader of Latin America because nobody asked me to be that. I do believe, though, that Brazil's greater representation is based on its political and economic weight. Needless to say, I need no encouragement to defend Latin America. I defend it because that is what I believe in.

I asked Lula da Silva what kind of situation involving Brazil could take place for the benefit of Latin America. The Brazilian President said that the region needs to be strengthened, and for that, it would be great if his country and Argentina could understand each other better. He adds: "Everything would be easier that way. What is really needed is for Brazilians and Argentinians to leave aside those small disputes and historical vanities and to sit side by side like two great countries. There are residues of historical preconceptions, from the times when Collor de Mello and Carlos Menem would argue who was closest to George H. W. Bush. Kind of: 'I had two coffees with him at my country house. — Well, I had three.' Argentina and Brazil really do not need that. Argentina needs to be strong and sovereign, Brazil needs to be strong and sovereign and we will do well when we stop seeing each other as adversaries and start thinking of each other as allies. We need to respect our sovereignty and be more constructive in the consolidation of political alliances."

In his analysis, Lula mentions George H. W. Bush, ex-president of the United States. Why has that country had so much influence in the countries of Latin America? Regarding US intromission, how much of that responsibility lies in the hands of those Latin American countries? Lula is categorical: "There are a lot of people that say 'we are poor because of United States imperialism', but American imperialism only had terrible influence in some countries because their elite was terrible. If the elites were more honest, and fought for sovereignty, the *coup* against Manuel Zelaya in Honduras would never have occurred, and the *coups*, decades ago, in Argentina, Brazil, Paraguay and Uruguay would have never occurred either. Before, Brazil and Argentina would only look up to the United States or Europe; and Venezuela, Colombia, Bolivia or Ecuador would only look up to the United States. I, who have been the most important union leader in Brazil for over ten years, was never invited to go to any country in Latin America! But every month I would go to Europe."

The region's current outlook is different. But, what was it like, the road that led us to a change in direction? What decisions was the President of Brazil able to make to stop the dependence on the United States? Lula explains: "My first term started on 1 January 2003. On 10 December I went to visit George W. Bush, President of the United

States. When I got there, I realised that all that man talked about was the war with Iraq. And I would tell him: 'Mr President, I have got nothing against Iraq. My war is not against Iraq; my war is against hunger, against the poverty of my country.' He was almost trying to get Brazil involved in that war with Iraq. What did Brazil have to do with Iraq? We knew there were no chemical weapons there, because the President of the Commission was a Brazilian man who later became ambassador in London, and he literally said that there were no chemical weapons in Iraq. I came back to Brazil with two convictions: First, we needed to put an end to FTAA (Free Trade Area of the Americas); second, we needed a shift in our perspective. On 3 January 2003, I went to the World Economic Forum in Davos, and when I got back, I said to our Foreign Affairs Minister, Celso Amorim: 'We need to change the world's political and commercial geography. We cannot continue to have things the way they are. We need to look to South America.' The stages had to be: First, the Mercosur; then, South America; then Latin America; and later Africa, Asia and the Arab world. We had to prioritise those countries in our relationships."

Lula da Silva said that, within six years, the relationship of South America with Africa and the Middle East had been greatly increased. And he added that for the regional integration to be consolidated, institutions are needed — institutions that would guarantee democratic decisions. He said that his country has already proposed that the region should have, among other things, its own Defence Council and a Congress for the fight against drug trafficking.

A Portrait of the President

Luis Marinho is Mayor of São Bernardo do Campo, in São Paulo. He tells us: "I met Lula at the union. I was a worker at Volkswagen and he was President of the union. He was always leading mass meetings of workers at the company's doorstep, talking about the needs of the struggle, going on about the problems — and what he said captivated, conquered and affected the people. He was one who convinced the workers." Conceição Farias, a member of the Municipal Directory of the Partido dos Trabalhadores of Recife, tells her own experience with Lula: "I could say that I voted for Lula as Federal Deputy against the will of my ex-husband, who does not even know. He wanted me to vote Paulo Maluf, and he put up a giant poster of him right in front of my house. But I was not going to vote for that scoundrel who calls my president a 'bearded toad'. So I voted for Lula." João Paulo Lima da Silva, member of the National Directorate of the PT, says: "I think Lula will be remembered for the courage he showed in his commitment to the people. He is the great revolutionary of the Brazilian people. A revolution without weapons. A revolution without dictatorships. A revolution that respected the adversaries and even the class enemies."

And he gets excited: "We need to build, not waste, the twenty-first century. We have already lost the twentieth century. We have to seize the twenty-first century. And that is only possible in peace, democracy, with strong constitutions and with great social policies. And it is important to invest a great deal in education — a really great deal. I mean, with fifteen or twenty years of investments in education you can make the greatest revolution a nation could ever need. And that is what we are doing in Brazil."

Lula's statements invite us to reflect on how the current Brazilian model could be defined. Before explaining his ideas, Brazil's President says that he is sure that Brazil is not inclined to the so called twenty-first century socialism, and laughs. After the laughter, he explains how Brazil works since his arrival to power and why.

I had a commitment. I had to prove that I was fitted to govern the country, and for that matter, I assumed some commitments, as a mother would. Let's take, for example, a mother from the peripheries of Buenos Aires, Argentina, who has eight children. She loves them all, but she will always give special care to the one who is more debilitated. The weakest is not the prettier, or the smartest, but the one in greatest need. That is the spirit of a mother — and that is how I want to govern Brazil. We need to take care of the poorest, because the richest do not need the Government. That is the truth! The rich man, when he looks for a leader, he wants a thousand billions, two thousand billions, three thousand billions in financing. The poor man, when he looks for a leader, he wants ten pesos, fifty pesos, fifty reals, fifty dollars. That is, the simplest thing in the world is to govern for the poorest part of the country — it is the simplest thing, and I chose that option. And with that, one becomes renowned in the poorest parts of the country; one can go to the poorest parts and people will know that we are taking care of them. And what we are doing is still too little. We need to do a lot more. For example, what we are doing with education will be noticed by people only ten or fifteen years from now. We have built 214 new professional technical schools, when in the previous hundred years only forty had been built. We have built two new universities, one of which is the Afro-Descendent University: half African students, half Brazilian students. This is our great legacy. The model which whoever comes next must surpass. I think we will continue to work and I want people to know that whoever follows in power will have to do more, never less. He or she will have to take more care of the people, treat them with more respect. The basic idea is the following: "Brazil is yours. I am merely a unionist from Brazil; you are the inhabitants. So, please, help us decide what it is that you need us to do."

An important issue of the last few years is the international crisis that took place as a result of financial speculation. I ask Lula what is his opinion on what triggered the crisis and what will be its consequences. Lula considers: "I think it is more of a responsibility of the richest countries than ours. The crisis blew up in 2008, but it had been building up in all the levels of financial speculation that went through the global financial system. Nobody can make money without producing a result, or a material thing. I cannot sell you a piece of paper that you will sell to someone else, and he will sell it again and so on — that is fifty people making a profit out of a paper that only produced one piece. It is not possible. I think that this crisis revealed just how rotten the global financial system is — and, above all, how rotten the market is. I lived in the eighties and the nineties, times when the All Mighty Market God could do anything. The Market God was going to solve education problems, unemployment, and any other problem the country could have. But the Market God failed, because when he was needed, he did not know what to do. And then, the State had to intervene in order to save the economy. The crisis also called the attention of everyone who made it possible for the State to have an important role once again. I do not want a manager State or a business State; I have a vocation for an instigating, controlling and regulatory State. The Government has to regulate the financial system."

A Different January
On 1 January 2011, Luiz Inácio Lula da Silva was to become ex-President. He said that he would feel really sad that day, because it was to be the

first day since the return of democracy that he would not be able to present himself for election. He added: "I think people will miss me a little bit when they go to vote. I am preparing myself for January second, because I will wake up with no one to curse, no one to pick up the phone for me. I will live a quiet life, because I do not wish to give ideas — I have no right to tell whoever wins the elections how he or she should act. I will finish my term and whoever comes should have the freedom to do the things he or she thinks are better. I think my work is done. I will end my term being sixty five years old, and I think it is time I take it easy now."

And how would you like to be remembered by future generations? What are the history books going to say about your two administrations? Lula imagines: "I would like to be remembered as the President that did the most for the social movement of this country — but it is difficult to imagine what will be said about me in ten or twenty years' time. I'd rather not get my hopes up. I wish somebody from our own space will replace me, and that he or she does twice as much as I did. And in that way I will be forgotten, it is simple. Leaving the Presidency behind is the only thing I want; to walk down the streets and let everyone call me *'compañero'* — colleague — like they used to call me, and for me to be able to treat people as *compañeros* too. So I would like to see my Presidency as a stage in my life, and that now I am going back to living a normal life, wishing to have beers with my friends or play cards. I would also like to participate in some meetings of the metal union. I am going to keep on thinking — I still have a good head for that. I only want not to work anymore!"

Lula laughs. All the while I have been sitting in front of him I saw a poor child who started working too early, a union member that did not want to go into politics, an active president, a leader central to Latin American life. Lula was all those things as we spoke, and he never stopped smiling, having fun, getting emotional, and reflecting. Before we shake hands, he asks me for the time to give a last message to the Latin American people. He says: "We are not poor because God wanted it so; we are not poor because of the United States or Europe. We are poor because, for centuries, even after the Spanish, our elite still continued to be undemocratic, still unfair with the distribution of the riches produced in the country. We need to decide which is the country that we want to have, which is the continent that we want to have — because, either we decide it and we construct, or we will get nowhere.

I have my hopes up; I have faith in the role Latin America will play in the twenty or thirty years to come. But, in order to get there, we need to work really hard, with great democracy, with great peace, with great social participation and great distribution of the capital to improve the life of the people. Because that is what matters. I think there is a magnificent democratic revolution in Latin America — with its virtues and its flaws — but the people are moving because they understood that what there was before was no good. And the people expect improvement. The poorest are starting to lift their heads up — that is what made me win the 2006 elections. And the responsibility grows, because when the political left gets to power, it does not get there to make speeches — we came here to govern!"

CHILE: MICHELLE BACHELET
A WOMAN IN LA MONEDA

Verónica Michelle Bachelet Feria was born in Santiago de Chile, on 9 September 1951. She went into exile from 1975 to 1979. She graduated as Paediatric Surgeon with a major in Epidemiology in 1982. In 1990 she joined the Public Health System, hired as an Epidemiologist at the West Metropolitan Health Service and later at the National Commission on AIDS. At the same time she worked as an advisor to the World Health Organisation, to the Pan American Health Organisation and to the German Agency for International Cooperation. In 1996 she was chosen to be a member of the Central Committee of the Socialist Party. In 1998 she worked as an advisor to the Ministry of Defence. In 2000 she took over the Health Ministry during the presidency of Ricardo Lagos, and in 2002 she left it to take over the Ministry of Defence. Between 2006 and 2010 she was President of Chile for the Concentración Nacional party. Bachelet was re-elected in December 2013 and her term will end in 2017. She has three children and is divorced.

The *Palacio de La Moneda* (The Coin Palace), the seat of government in Chile, has a tragic story. On 11 September 1973, the Army and the Air Force bombed the building as part of the plan Augusto Pinochet had to overthrow Salvador Allende, the socialist president who had won the elections in 1970. Allende died in the attack and Pinochet got to power. Furthermore, priceless treasures of Chilean history were lost — among others, the Declaration of Independence of 1818 and Bernardo de O'Higgins' original badge, which was a star-shaped piece that was placed on one end of the presidential sash. For the first time in Chilean history, a *coup-d'état* broke with the institutional order.

La Moneda (the abbreviation for the Palace in Chile) is different now. Democracy returned in 1990, and the fourth presidency since then was in the hands of a woman. Michelle Bachelet recounted her feelings as she entered the building as President: "The first time I entered *La Moneda* as President, on the one hand, I could not help remember everything that had happened there, but, on the other hand, I had that feeling that made me think: 'I am the first woman; all the eyes of Chile are on me, and many eyes of the world too. I have the responsibility of doing things right.' I had that feeling, that is always with me — the feeling of duty; feeling the necessity to give the people what they need, what they hoped for... to fulfil the expectations and the confidence deposited in me. And I think that this was the most important thing to me in those first days. Then, of course, many times it was contrasted with going around the different offices, where so much happened."

Before becoming President, Michelle Bachelet was Minister of Defence during the administration of Ricardo Lagos. At that time, her entrance to the Palace of *La Moneda* had some curious connotations. Bachelet says: "I was experiencing a special moment as a person that gathered, like I say as a joke, all the possible sins for institutions that sometimes tend to be more conservative. You have to have in mind that I am a woman, of course, but also a socialist, a divorcee and an agnostic — characteristics that sometimes are not the best calling card to work with some sectors. But, on the contrary, it turned out to be a wonderful relationship all through my Minister of Defence days."

For Bachelet, her presence in *La Moneda* relates, above all, to an enhancement of memory and the respect for human rights. "We cannot forget the past — says Michelle — if we want to have a solid future. And in that respect, we have worked hard during these years. Standing on the past so as not to repeat the errors, to have memory, bring up the truth — but also looking to the future."

Once, Bachelet said she had no responsibility for what had happened during the dictatorship years, but she did have a responsibility not to let it be repeated. It is a remark that made a great impact on me, and for that, I asked her to expand: "Ever since the Lagos administration we have worked on a conception of human rights policy based on the phrase 'there is no tomorrow without a yesterday'. And there is no truth, besides, if there is no justice and reparation. It is very important to know the truth about what has happened. Because, beyond the particular incident of '73 and the following years of brutal violations of human rights, throughout our history, every time we have put our differences on the table and have not been able to solve those differences in a democratic way, situations have arisen that we have come to regret. And these situations have meant too much pain and too much sadness to our people."

Bachelet argues that the way out of this is to look for and understand the diversity that enriches Chilean society; that there can be big differences but that does not mean we have to look at the others as enemies. Regarding this, the President says that in every human rights policy she was involved in, this understanding has been sought after. She explains it like this: "We have created the conditions — in my style of leadership — to preserve memory, so that we do not forget — to be able to look to the future with a constructive view and to avoid the mistakes of the past. But also, on the other hand, having in mind that if we do not want to leave unaddressed challenges we have to build the country together. The central issues — that are State Policy — have to last forty, fifty or seventy more years."

For Bachelet, the building of a future without forgetting the past has to be done with a specific view of human rights, but also with a view that implies acting day by day on long lasting policies — and having in mind diversity. "Diversity enriches us. And when I say diversity I mean ethnic diversity, diversity of gender, of age, of religion, of sexual orientation, and political diversity — undoubtedly. And in this manner, in my opinion, one consolidates democracy. Because I do not think that democracy is just about choosing. Democracy is also built every day, opening up places for participation to more people."

No Revenge

Michele Bachelet did not only suffer the consequences of the dictatorship as a Chilean citizen, but also at a deeper personal level. Her father, Alberto Bachelet, was a General in the Air Force. In 1973, he refused to take part in the *coup* against Allende — he was head of the *Junta de Abastecimiento y Precios* (Committee for Supply and Prices) of Allende's administration. He was detained and released several times by the dictatorship, until he died in 1974 of a heart attack, product of the constant torturing he was subjected to.

Personality Report

Julia Alvarados Thimeos, headmistress of the N°1 Javier Carrera School, which Michelle Bachelet attended, shows a book that contains the grades, marks, and personality reports of the students who graduated in 1969. Among those names is Michelle Bachelet Jeria. So Julia reads the report on Michelle: "Strong and well defined personality. She adapts to the class and the school. Respectful and wonderful classmate. She has represented her school very well where she had to. President of her class. Very good performance in her studies. She has the conditions to succeed in her aspirations. Besides being intelligent, she shows interest in overcoming difficulties, making big efforts and being persevering. Signed: Head Teacher."

Alberto was the descendant of French immigrants, and he liked camping, going out for hunts and taking photos. Also, he had participated in literacy campaigns and in plans for stimulation of fish consumption. He also collaborated in the coordination for the aid to victims of the earthquake of 1960. It was there where he met Salvador Allende. His daughter Michelle remembers him like this: "I am just like my father, in the sense that he was always a very patriotic man — a man with great conviction in his ideas. But, besides, he was super open to dialogue. He was a very educated man. At home, a lot of reading took place; we would talk about culture, have debates. And my father was a very cheerful person, a good-humoured man, I would say. Very serious while at work, but always in good spirits."

When Alberto died, her daughter was 23 years old and she supported the Socialist Party — which was proscribed and had to go into secrecy. However, she was detained in 1975, along with her mother, Ángela. Separated and isolated, they were tortured for a month. Some weeks after that, they were set free and Michelle was able to leave the country.

The story helps me introduce a complex topic to the President of Chile: How do you manage to have a human conception — without revenge in your thoughts — when you have to make State policies regarding such sensitive matters? What is the personal process by which one can dissociate both things? The answer: "I do not have the feeling that it is a dissociation and I will tell you why. I get this same question from the families of political prisoners, of disappeared detainees, of executed people. They ask me: 'What is the magic formula?' Because, besides, they tell me that they see me in peace. There is no magic formula; I wish I could give you that formula. One explanation I find is that, precisely, when one has seen what has happened to one's people, when one has many dear friends that have been executed, disappeared, thrown in jail, gone into exile, missed their parents' funeral because they were not allowed to enter — well, with so much accumulated pain, one has to say: "I do not want this ever to happen again to my children, my grandchildren, or the great grandchildren of anyone in this country."

Bachelet says that in order to have these ideas materialised in definite State policies, truth, justice and reparation have to be recovered and we must learn to solve conflicts in a democratic way. If it is not done in that way, then all we are doing is to reproduce models of intolerance. For Michelle, it was due to intolerant visions that many

Chileans started to think of others as enemies.

The President thinks that her ability to mitigate pain comes from her family environment. She recounts: "In our case, my mother and I took the pain of the losses we have had, as a society and as a family, towards a more positive attitude, more constructive. I know that in psychology it is called resilience, which is the capacity to bounce back even stronger after suffering great pain instead of being neutralised. In psychology there are two types of anguish: paralyzing anguish and mobilizing anguish. Everyone, when faced with a challenge, experience some anguish, but of the useful type — it is that adrenalin that keeps us moving forward to find answers. I think that when human beings are overcome by fear, or by that paralyzing attitude, or by the desire for revenge, we do not move forward — neither as individuals nor as a society."

Even though her family is "highly resilient", as she herself puts it, Bachelet confesses that there are situations that really move her. She remembers, for example, an act in which Joan Turner — Victor Jara's English widow — was granted Chilean nationality. "I think it is an act of justice — says Michelle — for a woman that fell in love with Chile; falling in love, first with a great choreographer, Patricio Bunster, and then with Victor Jara. Those kinds of things still move me deeply."

Alleviating the Pain
Following, some questions that arise regarding Michelle Bachelet's involvement in politics, being a doctor and coming to power:

How did this woman who went to Medical School and had a military father get into politics?

Injustice still hurts and that is the reason I got into politics. I did not get into politics because I had read four books and convinced myself that it was necessary to make the world a better place and devote myself to public service. On the one hand, my family taught me, almost since I was wearing diapers, about public service — about being there for the rest. But, on the other hand, for me, being in politics is about fighting injustice. I rise against injustices, against the idea that there is a "natural order of things" that establishes that there will always be poor and rich people. I do not believe it to be that way. I think that this world has to be built by us, and we need to aim at a better world, a better country, a better region for every citizen. And I will be onto that until the day I die. When I chose to follow a career in Medicine, I thought it out in the same way — in trying to alleviate the pain. It has to do with this thing about trying to relieve people from their pain, about supporting them and about helping to find solutions. A lot of people ask me: "What does Medicine have to do with politics?" My brother would ask me: "Why, after seven years in university and three years to specialise in paediatrics, are you dedicated to public health?" And I have always felt that there was no contradiction in that. There is a direct correlation between politics and medicine, in that they both, ultimately, seek to solve problems and improve the living conditions and well-being of the people. I believe them to be remarkably correlated.

Has your previous experience as a doctor given any special characteristic to your presidency?

I do not know whether it is because of my previous practice as a doctor or because of the reasons why I came to be a doctor — and particularly paediatrics. I love being in touch with people. This has helped me, both as a Minister and as President, when it came to decision making: I make decisions with deep knowledge of the subject. It is not enough for me to be told "this", or that a minister suggests me "that". I study the subjects, consider the options — I try to have my own appreciation of the subject at hand, and then I make a decision. And I have had to study subjects, previously unimaginable to me, that were really fascinating. I do not hope to be an expert on every subject; that would be excessive arrogance. But I do expect to be as sure as I can that the decision is made, so to speak, covering as much ground as possible. And in that respect, that has to do with precision in looking for remedies that are better than the sickness — my previous experience as a doctor has had a great influence.

When was the first time you thought you could become President?

I would say that it did not cross my mind when I was young — rather, if someone had told me ten years ago that I was going to be the President of the Republic, I would have burst into laughter. In fact, I started studying military matters because I thought that, given the political history of our country, one of the problems had been the lack of political dialogue, real dialogue, between the world of politics and the world of the military. The political world, in general, paid no attention to military matters — it was not taken much into account — and, therefore, only a few times were there valid interlocutors as perceived by the military world. But all that had to do with the handling of power. I was the first woman to become Minister of Health in Chile. However, nobody thought of me as a possible President back then. It was only when Lagos named me Minister of Defence. That is to say, that position was more related to power. I think I had performed correctly, and just then it became something imaginable to think of a woman as a candidate for the presidency. To be honest, I had not set out for it — let alone made it my goal — until I had to really think about it when the polls started to show, overwhelmingly, that the people wanted me to be the next President of the country.

In that moment, when the possibility came up to become President, did it cause any kind of unease having to make the decision?

Two things happened to me. On the one hand, there is this characteristic of mine, completely inherited from my mother, that is brutal realism. I do not fall for fairy tales. I have an intuition as to how things will develop. And my feeling was that, being the first woman, the expectations were going to be much higher than the actual possibility to fulfil them — no matter how well I performed. I was aware of the brutality that implied coming to power with such high expectations and of the fact that it would demand a lot of work from me, but also that those expectations could easily fall apart for many people. So, I was aware, so to speak, of that. On the other hand, the other great fact was that if I was to become the first woman to be President of Chile, there would be this big weight on my shoulders, this big responsibility towards women and to the future of women in politics — not just here, but in many other places where they saw it as a novelty that Chile would elect a woman to become President. I knew very well the burden that was on my shoulders — the responsibilities. A friend of mine had told me: "I suggest you do this only if you believe you are going to have a good time", not in a festive kind of way, but in the sense that if I was going to do it, I had to enjoy it, the good and the bad, with enthusiasm and not go around thinking "what have I gotten myself into". Although I must admit I have asked myself that question at some point. All I hope for is not to fall short of expectations.

Life in Pictures

Michelle Bachelet's mother, Ángela Jeria, makes a profile of her daughter through photographs, memories and reflections: "When Michelle was young, she was a hippie — not so much in the way she used to dress but in the way she used to think. Since she was a child, she proved to be very smart, very responsible and she did not aspire to become the best of her class. At the same time, she could sing — she formed a choir with her classmates and they even went on television. Michelle was like that." She shows a picture of Michelle as a child. She also points at a picture of Michelle wearing the Presidential sash, and says: "She looks beautiful in that one." She continues: "On Saturdays, my husband would be home, sitting on his sofa, reading his newspaper. Michelle was very little, and I can picture her crawling up his father's legs with her bottle. She would lie down on his father's paper and have her bottle, and I think, for her, it was a sort of refuge. My husband was an exceptional man."

The *Concentración* as a Model

Chilean political experience over the last twenty years is something unique in Latin America. Since 1990, the country was governed by the *Concentración de Partidos por la Democracia or* Coalition of Parties for Democracy (also known, in Spanish, simply as the *Concentración)* — a coalition that gathered almost all of the opposition to Pinochet's dictatorship and that is formed by parties of different political backgrounds. Having this in mind, the Chilean model is often referred to as a model to follow. What is the secret that sustains the *Concentración?* Bachelet reflects:

> A very important part has to do with its origins. We have to bear in mind that one sector of the *Concentración* had been opposing each other even during Allende's administration. The Christian Democrats were in opposition, but the socialists and the radicals were in government. And an alliance was formed — an alliance that, to different parts of Europe, escapes understanding. If you go to Spain, the People's Party and the Socialist Worker's Party stand in different corners. In some countries there are electoral alliances, but there is no project like the *Concentración*. What bind us together are the hardships we had to endure regarding the loss of liberties. I mean, the *Concentración* takes the substantial and the essential and

prioritises it, pushing that which makes us different into the background. The essential values are common to all of us. I would say that the fight for freedom and the recovery of democracy were central. But also, in the process, a conviction started to grow — a conviction that the country needed a model that would allow us to take a leap towards development, growth and equality. To govern is also to be capable of putting together different drives and wills in favour of an idea, a project, a programme. What was essential to the *Concentración* was having the main goal on target all the time, and that goal is to keep on working to give Chile a democratic project with governability. A fairer, more supportive, more humane and more integrated Chile. I think we share that idea in the *Concentración*.

If the *Concentración* is clearly a model unique to Chile, unrepeatable and exclusive, is there also a socioeconomic model that is exclusively Chilean? Is there an exclusive Chilean model, for example, regarding State performance? Bachelet says that she is not sure whether there is an exclusive model for Chile. What she points out is the decision, once democracy was recovered, to reinsert the country in the political world, which was then under a new context — globalisation — which also required a sort of connectivity in communications and in markets.

Michelle thinks that a key feature in Chile's politics was the ability to see the opportunities that globalisation could bring with open economic policies. She adds: "I think Chile decided to go with a model that had solid macroeconomics, greatly based on exports and investments, with tax responsibility, but having in mind that growth has to go hand in hand with equal opportunities and social justice — that there is no need for an exchange. The *Concentración* has always aimed at harmonious development — meaning, that it includes, it does not exclude. I am talking about regions, gender, age, ethnic groups. Inequality in our societies is not only economic. To strongly believe that it is possible to grow in order to include and to include in order to grow; and that it is not just an ethical factor, or a political element or of social justice — it is all those things, but it is also an economic factor. Because if you have workers in good conditions, that are properly trained and well educated, those are also a factors that make your project more competitive. Everyone wins if you start seeing things that way."

Brazil: "Lula" Da Silva

Happiness According to Chile

In the nineties, a German political expert and Chilean nationalised citizen said that Chilean society was doing much better than during the dictatorship times of Pinochet, but, however, it was not a happier society. There was a sort of disenchantment, because access to other goods came with profounder and more complex demands. What should the Government do given such paradox? Bachelet has a peculiar understanding of this topic: "It has something to do, I suspect, with Chilean identity. Here in Chile we tend to see the glass half empty instead of the glass half full. And also, we get very excited and happy when we accomplish something, but three minutes later it becomes part of the landscape. When I was a Minister for President Lagos, he would tell me: 'But that is progress, Michelle.' And he was right. When you accomplish something you want other things. But I believe there is also a cultural thing."

One of the projects that was carried out during Bachelet's administration was the creation of a space called *Imagen País* — a foundation that shows Chile to the world, so that everyone has a chance to get to know it better. Michelle says: "One of the questions we asked ourselves was: What are we, Chileans, like? What is our identity?" And she answers that question with an anecdote: "A friend of mine was ambassador in a country of the Caribbean which had a high poverty rate, but, to his surprise, people was very happy. And he asked his driver: 'How come everyone is so happy in spite of all your problems?' And the driver answered: 'Apart from being poor, you want us to be miserable and not enjoy ourselves?' Well, that is a completely different culture to the Chilean. Every study shows that Chileans are not happy. Even though they have a higher development rate than some other countries, these countries are happier. I think this has many variables, and one of those variables is that, for a long time, we were — as a country — like an island, the world's edge, a long and narrow country that had little connection with the rest of the world. And I think, maybe, that a certain quality emerges from that context. As a country, we are extremely demanding towards ourselves and towards our authorities — we always want more. It is all right, it is legitimate and it is part of the progress. I only wish that one day we will keep on working on our country and feel, not only happy, but filled with joy."

The topic leads us to the question of how are Chilean citizens regarded in other countries — especially in the rest of Latin America.

Brazil: "Lula" Da Silva

Michelle Bachelet says that a few years ago her compatriots were seen as too arrogant. She recounts: "It happened to me, that while I was attending international courses, people would tell me that I did not look like a Chilean, because all the Chilean that had taken the course previously were annoying and arrogant. But Chile has never been a country of arrogant people. We are a much simpler, stripped-down country, and we have a tendency to always speak in *chiquitito* (*i.e.* to add the diminutive suffix to the word). For many years, something that was really painful was said about us: that we were the best student but the worst classmate. However, what I can say from my experience being in positions of power, both during my time as a Minister with Lagos and during my Presidency, is that a lot of effort has been put in trying to convince everyone that integration is a key element — an element that will help us to continue to work very closely with the other countries of the region."

So, leaving aside the Chilean idiosyncrasy — what is the relationship between Chile and Latin America like? Bachelet thinks her country has always encouraged the unity of the region and that Chile has been very active with regards to integration matters. She adds: "We have managed, during my presidency and with the help of every country, to get the South American Council of Health and the South American Defence Council off the ground, as part of the work we were carrying out at UNASUR and, in particular, in Chile. And as we strongly believe in UNASUR, we also believe that Latin America, as a whole, represents a point of view that we need to keep on strengthening — and the Caribbean too. So, I would say that we do not want to be and have never been the worst classmates." A personal anecdote finds its way into the conversation: "I, for one, have tried to be a very good classmate. In high school I would win the "Best Colleague Award" among my friends, and I found it to be the best award, because anyone can get good grades." And Michelle laughs at her analogy.

I tell Bachelet that if there was a medal for the best colleague in Latin American countries, a great merit for that medal would have been the swift call made by Chile to the countries of UNASUR when Bolivia's institutional stability was in danger, back in 2008. The President remembers it as follows: "It was a very important incident; that is why we called up a meeting here in *La Moneda*. I think it has proved that UNASUR is an important group and it can help a lot. Processes can be supported and accompanied when the corresponding parts agree to that. I always tell the Presidents of this region: 'We cannot *farrear* this historical moment.' *Farrear*, in the Chilean lingo, is to miss a chance to do something."

Michelle's Marks

Michelle Bachelet reached the end of her term in office in March 2010. A few months earlier, when we had this meeting, I had asked her how she thought she was going to be remembered. And she told me: "My main concern has been how to create better conditions to make people feel safer in the context of the vast difficulties of the modern world. I would say that the government's global hallmark is social protection. And there has to be a better Government — an efficient Government that will guarantee public goods for the people; a government that is there for the people, willing, and that is capable of solving the flaws of the market. The State has to generate equality. For example, there will always be sectors that will want to privatise CODELCO, Chile's copper company, and I have said it many times: 'Not a chance; not during my term.'"

The future that is waiting for Bachelet, now no longer President, is a future of much less responsibility. She pictures it this way: "The only thing clear to me is that wherever I happen to be, I will be a citizen with concern for the motherland, working at the service of others. I have not had time to think exactly what it is that I will be doing. I am a simple person and I will continue to be one. Whatever I have had, has always been because of my work. And I will continue to work. But I can imagine that this change in pace, the lack of adrenalin, must be hard. I will have to run around the house to use all my energy in some way. I will obviously find a job — I am still young to retire. And I will have to pay the enormous time debt I have with my family, my son, my grandson."

I ask her if she could share with me a collective dream for Chile's future and she tells me that she hopes for "a country ever more united, more caring, more humane and fairer."

So be it.

Colombia: Álvaro Uribe
Of Guerrillas and Violence

Álvaro Uribe Vélez was born in Medellin on 4 July 1952. He is married to Lina Moreno Mejía and has two children. He studied law at the University of Antioquia and received a Certificate of Special Studies in Administration and Management from Harvard University in 1993, where he also specialised in Conflict Negotiation. In 1998 and 1999 he was Senior Associate Member at Oxford University in England thanks to the Simón Bolívar Scholarship of the British Chevening Scholarships programme. In 1976, Uribe was Chief of Assets for the Empresas Públicas de Medellín (Public Enterprises of Medellín). Between 1976 and 1978 he served as Secretary General of the Ministry of Labour. He was City Counsellor and Mayor of Medellin. Between 1986 and 1994 he was elected National Senator. In 1998, he was elected Governor of Antioquia. In 2002 he became the President of Colombia. He was re-elected in 2006 and his term came to an end in August 2010.

When you sat in front of Álvaro Uribe, President of Colombia, you sat in front of the man who governed the country that is the most concerned with violence in all of Latin America. It would also be true if I said that you sat in front of the first man that was this concerned about that issue. For thirty five years, the presence of the *Fuerzas Armadas Revolucionarias de Colombia* (Revolutionary Armed Forces of Colombia), or FARC, has been an inconvenience for every Colombian government due to its actions that are influenced both by guerrilla war and conventional combat. It is estimated that, in 2010, the FARC are present in twenty four of the thirty two departments of Colombia, and have as many as six thousand members. Their presence has also been reported in at least four other countries. The FARC are considered as a terrorist group by the Colombian government, although not every country in the region defines them that way.

Since the eighties, paramilitary groups that arose as a response to the actions of the insurgents have joined the stage. Besides these two groups, there is also the drug cartel, which is accused of having contact with the two other groups. Thus, a really violent combination emerges.

The hardship of the political and social situation is manifested clearly by each gesture, each word that comes out of Álvaro Uribe. That rigidity and that severity can be appreciated in the face of the Colombian President. His discourse and his goals seem to be influenced almost only by the context of that search for more and more security.

Like no other leader of the region, Uribe reflects upon terrorism and drug trafficking at all times. So, if from the outside Colombia is still regarded as a violent and dangerous country, what are the historical conditions that led up to violence, guerrilla and drug trafficking in Colombia? All throughout Latin America there have been histories of violence, but, why is it still persistent in Colombia? Uribe goes through the history:

The answer to that is a difficult one. There are a lot of decent books written about that. Fearing oversimplification, I would say this: Colombia is living the post-independence era. During the nineteenth century we had civil wars. The last one was the Thousand Days' War that was over by 1902. During that war there were over 100,000 casualties, and the country entered a huge depression. Panama, which — for me — was the crown's jewel, declared its independence. I would say that we had forty years of relative peace, but, during that time, the country developed a great fear over the exercise of authority. Halfway into the forties, in the twentieth century, the partisan guerrillas emerged. In some way, they shared some elements with the civil wars of the previous century because they demanded democratic liberties. Out of those partisan guerrillas came a very cruel period, but relatively short. When the Cuban revolution won, it ignited the Marxist ideological trend, the violent class struggle, the contemptuous attitude towards the rule of law. Every dream was destroyed and substituted only by a utopia — a utopia of a classless society. And so, Colombia left the partisan guerrilla era to enter the era of the Marxist guerrillas. Para-militarism appeared in the form of self-defence, and that competed in cruelty with the guerrillas. The guerrillas assassinated and kidnapped and tried to penetrate every strata of the society. Para-militarism did its part. And in the middle of this situation, drug trafficking became stronger, and then it happened that both the guerrillas and the paramilitary ended up being financed by the cartels. They took hold of drug trafficking and drug trafficking took hold of them. And this entire crisis was caused.

Uribe puts the emphasis of the current situation in the issue of drug trafficking and risks a diagnosis and his opinion on how to solve the problem: "First of all we need to stop the illegal drug trade, and that demands commitment from everyone. I think that there is an incorrect position towards drugs. Nowadays it is trending and it is all right to say that they need to be legalised, but, personally, I think that drugs become legal as permissiveness in consumption grows. What we need to do is to make that link of the chain — that is consumption — illegal. Also, we have lost sight of the impact that drugs have on the environment. Drugs may be a reason why the Amazonian trees are being cut down. We have to look at drugs from an environmental perspective, because drugs can be the greatest destroyer of the Amazon rainforest."

We go back to the particular issue of violence. Álvaro Uribe says that, years ago in Colombia, there was this fear to carry out security policies, because civility was regarded as weakness. But that feeling started to change when the security policies were adopted as democratic policies. He says: "That is why we have talked about democratic security, with democratic values, with freedoms, and I think this could help Colombia finally to overcome this crisis. And I would like to emphasise two things that are intangible. On the one hand, the Colombian government has regained the monopoly for fighting criminals. State justice had been usurped, de facto repealed in many regions. In the past, family disputes, fights between individuals, personal damage, homicides and other situations of the sort would be taken to the guerrilla leader or the paramilitary leader. But now, justice has been regaining territory. On the other hand, when I say that Colombia has been practising these democratic security policies we should not speak of ethereal forms of freedoms. Colombia has challenged, has stood up to the richest, most criminal and most dangerous terrorism in the world, with ordinary law, and not with martial law."

Uribe's discourse is firm and definite. He knows very well what he wants to say. However, in Latin America he might feel like a fish out of water. His vision regarding issues of security and terrorism is not quite shared among the other leaders of the region. Do you feel unacknowledged by other countries of the region because they do not share the same situation, or because they do not feel it as their own? Uribe answers: "Not unacknowledged, but I worry for them. Terrorism is treacherous and knows no frontiers. Today it may be killing Colombians but tomorrow it could be other countries. I do not feel that I am not being acknowledged, but we do need more cooperation.

Colombia: Álvaro Uribe

Because as long as Colombian terrorists see that they are not being chased with the same intensity outside Colombia, they will know they can hide elsewhere. And as long as they can hide, we are never, ever, ever going to see progress in the peace processes that are required. Peace processes that are not external to us."

The Colombian President's concern about fighting political violence has to do with more than his political position. He has, as well, a personal history. His father, Alberto Uribe Sierra, was murdered by the FARC in 1983, when he resisted an attempted kidnap. How does Álvaro manage to carry that personal experience in the context of the current Colombian situation? His answer: "I reflected a lot over that matter. The fact that my father was murdered leaves me with a sadness that will accompany me until the day I die. A sadness like no other. That is a problem that fifty per cent of the Colombian families have had to endure. So, when one looks at the country with the same eyes he looks at his children, he becomes immune to hate but totally sensible to the idea of changing everything so that the new generations will have a better chance. My generation has not lived one whole day of peace. The goal is to let the new generations enjoy permanent peace in a flourishing process that is in constant positive evolution."

Security

This obsession with feeling safe reaches every sector in Colombia. As President Uribe goes around the country with a wide array of security forces and communication forces, people from different spheres worry about the same issue. In Bogotá, a police officer says: "What President Uribe has done is to consolidate a public force presence in all the national territory." A taxi-driver who takes us through Bogotá says: "I think that security, in our day to day, has improved. The public force is constantly monitoring the city. From what I have heard on the news, the public force has already got to places that were off limits in the past because of the guerrillas." A street vendor, who is also a teacher, analyses: "Here we suffer from unemployment. And if unemployment rises, so does insecurity."

Uribe does not only criticise the FARC form a personal perspective. He also has a political vision of his own regarding the guerrillas in Colombia: "They have not set themselves firmly on the conscience of the people. They had imposed themselves by blood and fire. The guerrillas had proposed a fairer society and what they have accomplished is more unemployment and more poverty, and they have created, as a reaction, the paramilitary. The country then started a process of expansion of democracy, of popular elections of mayors and governors. But the insurgents — that days before had offered peace in exchange for measures in favour of the expansion of democracy — when the time came for those measures to be applied, they sent assassins that burst in, killing mayors and governors, and as coercion factors against the expression of democracy. Violence in Colombia has not been good for democracy, and least of all for social fabric. Terrorism becomes the main challenge for the rule of law, because you lose that very important element of culture that is the respect for the law, both by the leaders and by the citizens."

Politics

Álvaro Uribe got to power in a way he describes as "irrational", and, without a doubt, early. It is not a subject he is entirely comfortable discussing. This is the conversation we had when I was trying to ask him about his first steps in political activities:

In several interviews you have said that your insertion in the world of politics took place when you were very young...

It was irrational. I must not talk about that, because it was premature — it was before I could resort to the use of reason.

How old were you?

I cannot account for that. I do not even know now, I have been there all my life. One day, they asked my wife: "When is Álvaro going to start his campaign?" and she said: "He has never stopped campaigning."

But how did you get started?

Very small.
What is your first memory?

If you want me to tell you an anecdote...

Yes...

Colombia: Álvaro Uribe

In 1956 or 1957, the Colombian parties made an agreement called the Frente Nacional (National Front) in order to overcome violence and the government of General Rojas Pinilla. Furthermore, it was decided that a referendum would be called in order to adopt constitutional regulation, to adopt alternation and to recognise the political rights of women. My mother was one of the leaders of my region, and took me by the hand throughout that process. If you would ask me about my most distant memory about my irrational introduction to public life, I would refer to that one I have just mentioned.

And when did you let go of your mother's hand and started acting in politics out of your own will?

Also prematurely.

When was that? When was the first public event you went to without your mother?

I remember it was when I was ten or eleven years old, when I participated in political campaigns. But it was so irrational that there are some occasions when I do not feel like conjuring it up. However, I say this to the young ones, the most valuable resource is leadership — it is the most difficult to build and the most difficult to find.

That leadership you mention, have you inherited it? Is it intuitive? Did you realise along the road that you had it? Or do you need to study in order to get it?

The truth is that today there are probably hereditary factors, introduced factors. But in the end, it all comes down to studying. I think that in order to obtain leadership, one has to re-evaluate that old preconception that says that leaders are born. Today it is more important to understand that leaders are made. I would say that we have to end with that thing that makes us say: "The neighbour was born to be a leader, I was not." Today, leadership is based on three pillars: preparation, preparation, preparation.

When we leave aside those premature first steps in politics, Uribe seems to relax and is more open to make political analysis. I tell him that maybe a European decides to go into politics, and that is a decision he makes, as it could have been any other profession; but, in Latin America, to go into politics is to take a risk, because of the violent history that precedes and because of the conditions that are set in the public sphere. It could be said that that notion is exacerbated in Colombia. Is bravery something you need to have in order to go into politics? Uribe answers: "If you take politics only as a way of life and have no deeper commitments, then you have nothing to risk. If you go into politics with deep commitments and in countries like Colombia, you are going to have to take risks, undoubtedly. I have had three elements present at all times: always aim for public well-being and good faith; ask for God's protection; and also to remember Churchill: 'in democratic life, the only thing that is lost is that which is not risked.'"

I ask him if he is afraid because of the position he occupies. He tells me: "The only fear that must exist, besides the fear of God, is fear of fear itself. It is in human nature — that attachment to that precious gift that is life — but we need to face challenges with great effort and the first stage is to conquer fear."

The President of Colombia says that maturity in the exercise of power comes through commitment, and he adds that commitment has to be confirmed every day. "One has to call up one's self to duty every day," says Uribe. "One has to recruit himself every day."

Is it possible to ask for that kind of commitment of the younger generations? Is it possible to ask them to get involved and work for the construction of a different state of things? Álvaro Uribe thinks: "Undoubtedly. You can build a car factory, a university, and all those projects are feasible. But the toughest of all is the construction of leadership. We can run out of oil, but let us not run out of leadership. If there is leadership, it does not matter that we run out of oil. So, great leadership is indeed needed, and that leadership is finally expressed through political action of collective service. We have to encourage the younger generations to take that action, and that requires dedication, self-sacrifice and patriotism in the wide sense of the word."

State Policies

An important issue that the presidents of Latin America today have to face is — from various points of view — the role that the Government has to play after the era of neoliberalism. I ask Uribe about that, and he makes his point: "I think that Latin America has lived through the extreme and that that has to spawn reflections. It has lived through extreme neoliberalism that has dismantled the State. The state was murdered by decree, and that has caused a lot of damage. And then, the appearance of the inefficient bureaucratic State also caused great damage. And that, which looks like a game of antagonistic extremes, finally converges in one specific point: they both eliminate the State — neoliberalism eliminates the State by decree; bureaucracy and state control eliminate the State by suffocation. The first one makes the State disappear with a signature and the second one breaks it down. Therefore, these extremes must urge us to reflect upon the need of a State that can guarantee social clauses, that is at the service of the community and that regulates but does not become interference or a monopoly. I think that the lessons from the past decades can lead the way to a State that is in favour of the community and not subject to ideological whims."

In this respect, we could say that Latin America is living two different realities, because it has some great features of modernism and of State transformations that have been taking place over the last years, but it also has kept some of the hindrances of the nineteenth century like autocratic governments and patronage systems. It looks like a reprint of the idea of magic realism — different eras and different moments living together. And there are differences too in the relationship between Government and the community. Uribe has his own vision of how this relationship should be in the future:

This relationship has to be established through democratic rule, with great balance between participatory democracy and representative democracy. Plebiscitary democracies ignore a very important element of democratic control that is the mediation factor called representation. But when that representation is disconnected from its primary constituent, from participatory democracy, then that representation also comes to an end. I would say that Latin America needs a good balance between participative and representative democracy. To overcome crisis is only possible, in my opinion, in a competitive society; and the only thing that makes a society constantly competitive is the never-ending process of educational revolution. And I speak of educational revolution in the most comprehensive meaning of education: from childhood up to the greatest efforts of science. Education must be accompanied by democratic rule. Education can make our societies less dependent on primary riches exploitation and more dependent on productive innovations. When you see societies that become richer by making use of natural resources through primary activities without much added value, you can easily realise that that kind of richness is not sustainable.

Since 2008, the world has experienced a financial crisis of massive dimensions. For Latin American countries, it was paramount to decide how to distribute the resources at that time of crisis. How did Colombia manage to solve this situation under the administration of Álvaro Uribe? The President answers: "In this crisis we have found strengths and weaknesses. Among the strengths, we have augmented the country's reserves, the banking reserves, the deposit insurance, the savings; we have investor confidence. Among the weaknesses, exports that had greatly increased over the past years can now fall fifteen, eighteen or twenty per cent; we had been creating and regularizing jobs, but we now face bigger challenges in that respect. And that is why we have anti-cyclical policies. We are focusing on four main ideas: infrastructure, social protection network, protection of private investment projections, and public and private funding. Those four topics are duly measured. For example, regarding the social protection network, this year we must deliver 13 million daily meals to kids under five years old that attend school. When I came to power, they were delivering only 3.3 million."

I mention that some of the criticism made of Colombia was precisely that there were only citizen's security policies, and no social or economic ones. The President of Colombia answers: "Security and investor confidence create a state of prosperity that is the only atmosphere in which we can move forward with regards to social policies. And, at the same time, social policies are the only validator of security and investor confidence. Thus, the relation becomes transitive more than mutual. When we first started with the security policy, we knew that we could not get to every region only with the soldiers. So we came up with something called comprehensive accompaniment, comprehensive action. It is to get there with the soldiers, but also with education, with the improvement of electric energy, of the aqueduct, with families in action, with nutritional programmes, with microcredit. Of course there is a long way to go, but we are getting there."

Colombia: Álvaro Uribe

Álvaro: Student and Adversary

Carlos Gaviria Díaz was President of the Alternative Democratic Pole, which was an opposing sector to Uribe's administration, until 2009. In spite of that political distance, Gaviria Díaz was closer to Uribe than it is commonly imagined. He recounts: "I do not know if you know, but I used to be Uribe's professor at the university. I would say he was medium level to high. He was not the best, because he would split his time between his academic work, his political work and his business — because he used to work at a coffee shop. At that time, the university was going through a big process of leftward movement, and the assemblies, both of professors and of students, debated along the lines of Maoism and Trotskyism. But Uribe would suddenly start talking for the Liberal Directorate of Antioquia and people would start booing in a terrifying way. But he would wait for the booing to end and he would continue talking.

Regional Integration

Latin America is getting to its 200th independence anniversary. It is a good time to take stock of what has been accomplished in the continent and of the subjects that are still pending. What parts of what has been done would Uribe like to stress and what challenges does he think still lie ahead? The Colombian President says: "There is a huge consolidation of democracy and I would say there is material progress. There has been progress regarding integration. We still have great challenges with regards to security, competitiveness and the improvement of income distribution. I will make a future reference in light of Colombia's concerns, and extrapolate it to the rest of the region. Trust should be the first thing we ought to be seeking in Colombia. We think that Latin America has to build comprehensive, solid and permanent trust in the minds of his own people and in the minds of the rest of the world."

Regarding integration, it could be said that Latin America has the potential to move forward — thanks to its natural resources and its human resources — in the same direction that Europe moved when it formed the European Union. The question is whether the leaders of Latin America share that view. Is it possible for Latin America to grow stronger by joining efforts? Álvaro Uribe analyses: "Hopefully, it will happen. Recently, very important measures have been taken — like the integration of the Andean region to MERCOSUR (the Southern Common Market bloc). The European model for integration is a very important idea, because it has brought discipline to the macroeconomic management. There is no doubt about that. It has imposed respect for the democratic rules, and has stopped extreme governments from operating. No one in the European Union can move away from democratic rule. Democratic rule and European integration are obstacles for anyone who may take extremist positions of any kind. In that way, Europe has committed us all to fight terrorism."

The integration issue is central, but sometimes it seems there are more integrating institutions than real integration in Latin America. Uribe says he would like to put it in other words: "We have, today, more bureaucracy in the name of integration than actual integration. I think that some may have mistaken integration with the creation of bureaucratic organisations that have integration as their goal. We need more real integration and fewer bureaucratic organisations. For example, we often pass supranational regulations that we ourselves do not acknowledge. Thus, the institutions we have created to watch over and make sure these regulations are being obeyed end up being useless and expensive organisations."

When you find yourself being in Colombia, and thinking about its relationship with Latin America, it is inevitable to ask about Simón Bolívar, the decisive leading figure in the independence of Bolivia, Colombia, Ecuador, Peru and Venezuela. If Bolívar were watching us now from somewhere, would he be satisfied with the reality of Latin America? What would Bolívar say today? Uribe, who is a scholar in Latin American history and on Bolívar's thoughts, says:

Bolívar was an organised man. I think he had to make many decisions regarding institutions and that he did not make those decisions based on the impulses dictated by his ideological convictions but based on needs of those times. For example, he was not a centralist just because; he was a centralist because he understood that decentralisation would give place to local autocratic regimes that would oppose the fight for independence. I think that, today, he would worry about organisation — that has two major threats: terrorism that feeds on the drug trade and the temptation of state control that may be growing in some countries. He was a practical man. He promoted private investment, a revolutionary idea at the time. When we speak today about Latin America having to make great efforts in favour of research and development, we cannot forget that the Liberator's efforts in favour of development, for those times, were enormous — not to mention his idea of social cohesion that was consolidated all throughout the processes of Alto Peru and the origins of Bolivia, and that he would later apply when chaos tried to take hold of Nueva Granada (what today is Colombia). He was an integrator by vision and conviction.

August and Beyond

In August 2010, Álvaro Uribe's second term as President of Colombia came to an end. What was he going to do when he was done with his term? Uribe thinks and says: "I would like to gather with some friends and come up with a project for a university that has a frame of doctrine and convictions. I do not imagine myself away from political activity, but I do wish to take it more easily."

I then ask him where he is going to put all that passion for politics that he has since he was a boy. It is clear that academic life is more moderate than the political arena. The President answers me: "Passion needs to show results, not explosions. I would like a more result-committed passion rather than a passion committed to its expression." When will Uribe's wife be able to say that his campaign is finally over? He risks an answer: "Life will wisely take care of putting an end to my campaign."

In his first campaign, in 2002, Uribe won with 52 per cent of the votes. In 2006, he got 60 per cent. That shows the trust that the Colombian people have invested in him, but, how does he think the people of Colombia remember him after he was no longer President? What contributions does he think he has made? Uribe says: "I think our greatest effort was put into calling attention to the need of security — that is a democratic value and a source of resources, and not the way into a dictatorship. Also, we have called attention to the need for investments as an essential part of the budget for prosperity. And finally, we focused on social cohesion as opposed to the distribution of poverty."

To conclude, I asked him what he would like his children to say when, in the future, they are asked about their father. Uribe says that he hopes the will say the same thing he would put on his gravestone: "He never backed out."

Costa Rica: Oscar Arias
Declaration of Peace

Oscar Rafael de Jesús Arias Sánchez was born on 13 September 1940 in Heredia, Costa Rica. He studied Law and Economy at the University of Costa Rica. His graduation thesis for the Economy degree, "Pressure Groups in Costa Rica", won the National Price for Essays in 1971. In 1974, he got his Ph.D. in Political Science from Essex University in England. He was Minister of National Planning during the administrations of José Figueres and of Daniel Oduber Quiróz. In 1978, he was elected Deputy for the National Assembly. In 1987 he won the Nobel Peace Prize. He governed the country between 1986 and 1990 and started his second term in 2006. His term ended in 2010.

It is December 1948. José Figueres has won the Costa Rican Civil War and, as President of the *Junta de Gobierno,* makes a decision that was never seen before anywhere in the world. He dissolves his country's army. Meanwhile, an eight year-old boy gets to school to find out that Costa Rica no longer has an army. He does not understand what is going on, but he hears that over the past months there had been armed conflicts taking place. He has seen the police search his house and confiscated his father's cars. That boy is Oscar Arias, and he has no idea he will become President of Costa Rica or that he will win the Nobel Peace Prize.

Now, Oscar Arias is sitting in front of me and he analyses those events with his characteristic peacefulness: "What José Figueres did in '48 is the product of a visionary mind and a lot of courage, because, after a civil war, he became the first soldier ever to dissolve his army. He was convinced that a small country like ours, with limited resources, should not be spending money on weapons and soldiers."

Over sixty years have gone by, and Arias says that thanks to that measure, Costa Rica was able to redefine its priorities for the benefit of the society. The Costa Rican President says: "Our country spends 6.5 per cent of its gross domestic product in education and approximately 9 per cent on health care. At present, we are taking care of people's most urgent needs, and certainly, having an army is not one of those. What Costa Rica has done is to try and invest the dividends of peace in the most efficient way. How? Declaring peace to the world and hoping that their best defence was their lack of defence. Since then, nobody has dared to touch Costa Rica. And what we have accomplished is no utopia;

it is possible in any other place."

What Arias says is real. Because of his management, in 1991, Panama has also dissolved its army. "I always say that there is no safer border than the border between Costa Rica and Panama," says Arias. "Two countries with no army. Armies in Latin America had only been useful for *coups*, for repressing our people."

Arias is concerned with the search for peace settlements beyond the American limits. During his administration he proposed Palestine get rid of its army, and brought restlessness to many sub-Saharan countries. Results were not always as expected. Arias recounts: "More often than not, one tries unsuccessfully to talk countries into dissolving their armies, but the richer countries see this as an unpractical thing and too utopic, to put it mildly. If I were to put it harshly, it is because the weapon-producing countries want to continue selling weapons to poor countries to make them even poorer. Because that is the best way of perpetuating poverty: to spend money on weapons and soldiers instead of educating our children."

In 1987, Arias won the Nobel Peace Prize for his actions regarding the armed conflicts that took place in Central America during the eighties — especially for his opposition to the United States' support of the Nicaraguan *"Contras"* ("Counter"; as in *opposing*), that were groups against the Sandinista National Liberation Front. How did it feel, for you and for your country, to win the Nobel Peace Prize? He says: "At a personal level, it was a wonderful thing, because it is the most prestigious award in the world. But apart from me, it was of great significance to Costa Rica, because we put Costa Rica on the international map. For the first time ever, they heard about this country that had no army. Before that, nobody knew. For the first time they realised that we were a small oasis of democracy in the middle of an extremely conflictive Central America; and that caused national and foreign investments to rise, and tourism to rise too, and brought people from all over the world wanting to see how could there be a country with no army amid so much violence in America's waist."

I asked him if he remembers the exact moment when he found out he had won the Nobel Prize. Oscar Arias recounts it like this:

I was with my family — my children and my wife — on a beach in the Pacific. We had celebrated my wife's birthday and we were sleeping. It was around four in the morning. Suddenly, the walkie-talkies started to ring. We did not have any other means of communication because we were on a beach far away from San José. I picked up and my nephews told me that I had been awarded the Nobel Peace Prize. I really did not believe it for a truly obvious reason: I did not even know that I had been nominated. It was a very pleasant surprise. They then sent a small plane to pick me up, and when I got to the airport, all of my friends and everyone in the government were waiting for me. My mother was there too, waiting for me with tears in her eyes. José Figueres was there — he was already a bit sick — and he looked very proud and very happy. We all came over to the Presidential House and later I received a call from the Oslo Nobel Committee to tell me I had been chosen. They then sent me a letter and a telegram, which I have framed, because they are nice memories.

Formalities

Before we started the interview with Oscar Arias, the President was worried because his conversations were going to be transmitted in schools and he wanted to wear a suit. I told him it was not necessary, that the idea was to keep the conversations as informal as possible. Finally, an assistant convinced him to wear a jacket. After that occurrence, another conversation with one of Oscar Arias' assistants regarding formalities took place. It went something like this:

Assistant: Mr Senator, how would you like the President to address you?
Filmus: As Daniel, or Filmus.
A: If you want him to call you Daniel, he will call you Daniel. As you prefer.
F: He can call me Senator. Can I address him as Don Oscar?
A: Yes, no problem. How were you addressed by the other presidents you have interviewed?
F: I knew many of them for a long time. Some would call me Daniel, others Filmus.
A: None of them called you Senator?
F: Yes, Senator too.
A: How did Tabaré addressed you?
F: Filmus.
[Oscar Arias enters.]

Arias: Mr Senator or Daniel? Which do you prefer?
F: I prefer Daniel — the more informal the better. Can I call you Don Oscar?
Arias: Yes. Do you prefer me to call you Daniel or Mr Senator?
F: I prefer Daniel, but as you wish.

In his acceptance speech, Arias read the following verses of the Nicaraguan poet Rubén Darío:

Pray generous, pious and proud;
pray chaste, pure, heavenly and brave;
intercede for us, entreat for us,
for already we are almost without sap or shoot,
without soul, without life, without light, without Quixote,
without feet and without wings, without Sancho and without God

I mention to Arias that that speech and those words are very different from those uttered by the President of the United States Barack Obama when he received the same award in December 2009. Among other things, on that occasion, Obama said: "The United States of America has helped underwrite global security for more than six decades with the blood of our citizens and the strength of our arms. The service and sacrifice of our men and women in uniform have promoted peace and prosperity from Germany to Korea, and enabled democracy to take hold in places like the Balkans. We have borne this burden not because we seek to impose our will. We have done so out of enlightened self-interest — because we seek a better future for our children and grandchildren, and we believe that their lives will be better if others' children and grandchildren can live in freedom and prosperity. So yes, the instruments of war do have a role to play in preserving the peace."

Arias admits he finds it difficult to understand how they would give the Nobel Peace Prize to the President of the United States only nine months after he got to power and "actually having done nothing special." And he adds: "Obama's case and mine are very different — a military power like the United States and a country that voluntarily disarmed itself sixty one years ago. The United States' history is a history of war."

1986 was the first year Oscar Arias was in office. A year after, he managed to implement the "Arias Plan", that was created with the intention of bringing peace to Central America. How did that plan come up? Arias says: "To be honest, I had to differentiate myself from my main opposition that was Rafael Calderón Fournier. My party was part of the Government, we had to be re-elected ourselves, and it was not easy. Calderón had said that he would be on the same level as Ronald Reagan and, if it was necessary, he would send our Civil Guard to war. That really hit our tradition, all of our idiosyncrasy, our most cherished values shared among Costa Ricans. So I presented the peace plan. At first, it was met with widespread scepticism. The United States and the Soviet Union were against it; Fidel Castro too. It was necessary to create confidence in the plan; it was important that they realise that this peace plan was something all of my own, very personal, very Costa Rican — that I was not an instrument of Washington."

Arias tells me that he had to visit many Latin American presidents and also travel to Europe to convince Felipe González, François Mitterrand, Margaret Thatcher. For the President of Costa Rica, democracy was the key element of his plan for peace, the Arias Plan. "Democracy as a requirement for lasting peace in the region," Arias says. "That meant free elections. That is why Sandinistas were a bit sceptical at first. The Sandinista Movement had won the battle against Somoza in the mountains, and, like Fidel, expected no elections. It was hard. So much so, that no one expected that in August 1987 the five presidents would come to an agreement on that matter." But finally Costa Rica, Nicaragua, El Salvador, Guatemala and Honduras signed the agreement.

For Equality

Besides the fact that Costa Rica has no army, it has another singularity that differentiates it from many other Latin American countries: its level of inequality is much lower compared to the region's level. What is it that makes Costa Rica an example to follow regarding equality? The President says: "The level of social security is really high. Indeed, the most equalitarian countries in America are Costa Rica and Uruguay, and I think that what they both have in common is precisely that: great social spending. That equality does not come from the tax system. Nowhere in Latin America are taxes equitable or progressive. Rich people do not pay like rich people, and we know that. Maybe Brazil is an exception. If equality is not on the quality of the spending, the important thing is where it is aimed. In the case of Costa Rica, it is aimed, fundamentally, at culture, education and health. Besides, Costa Rican goods and services trade is equal to our country's gross national product, meaning that, compared to other countries, it has one of the most open economies in the continent. That is to say, Costa Rica is far from being a protectionist country, which is standard in most countries in Latin America."

Another aspect that often stands out about Costa Rica is its educational level. On that topic, Arias reflects: "The average length of schooling in Latin America still is around seven years, but ours is ten and a half. A compulsory and free education paid by the State since 1869. Our first Head of State, Juan Mora Fernández, was an educator, not a military."

Childhood and Politics

Many of the current Latin American Leaders admit never to have thought about being presidents until the opportunity was in reach. I ask the same thing to Arias and he answers: "When I was running for my first term and people would ask me about that, I would always say that the first time I ever thought about becoming president was in my mother's womb. It is a joke; but when I was in school, my classmates indeed teased me because I used to say that I wanted to prepare myself to become president. That came up in the yearbook once."

Where did that dream come from for little Oscar? He remembers it like this: "I dreamt of becoming president because of my father, who would give me many politicians' biographies — from Napoleon and Bismarck to Churchill, who was my hero since I was a little boy, and still is. At that time, when I was growing up, a great hero all around the world was De Gaulle. And then, during my time at the university in Boston, I met Jack Kennedy — I lived the 1959-1960 campaign of Richard Nixon and Jack Kennedy, and that had a great impact on me. And well, I decided to prepare myself. I met José Figueres, who was a very important ex-president and said to him: '*Don Pepe*, I want you to give me the chance to do something for my country in your future Government'. And he did. I was thirty years old when he appointed me Minister, and, ever since then, I have been involved with national politics in some way."

Young Arias did not think only about the Presidential Sash; he also liked football and books. He played for the school team and also swam.

But mostly, he studied — he was very interested in poetry and reading. His father had a very big library and forced him to write essays. Oscar would write them and send them to competitions. Hi tells this story passionately: "At some times I would win the first prize and at some others I would not win anything. The essays varied in theme, but mainly they were political essays. One of those essays required me to read a large part of Winston Churchill's memoirs, because it was about the World War and the Berlin Blockade in 1948. I also used to write for a magazine. We used to have here a magazine called *Combate* (*Combat*) that was run by a politician of my party.

Peace and other remedies
Francisco Rodríguez, Police Coordinator of the city of Heredia, in Costa Rica, tells us how the idea of peace is experienced in the inland regions. He says: "For any Costa Rican, peace means having no weapons. The police do not spend money on weaponry. In many cases, they are donated by other countries — some date back to World War II. The role of the police here is merely preventive. Costa Rica is a country that exports liberty principles." A coffee plantation worker at Café San Ramón expresses his opinion about daily life: "Life in the countryside is very difficult for us because salaries are too low. Don Oscar Arias does a lot in helping the poor, but I would like to have little piece of land I can call my own, so I can cultivate. I think the land should belong to he who cultivates it." A teacher from Ángeles Norte School tells her experience: "What really affects us is crime, mostly in the urban parts. Although here in Costa Rica that idea of the protective motherland is held — there is a lot of protection of the elderly and the younger — there is also, on the other hand, negligence in security and dwellings."

So, by the time I was eighteen I was already writing for magazines and for newspapers."

Once he was in the university, Oscar Arias wrote five books — all political analysis of Costa Rican reality. And he confesses he would like to write his memoirs once he retires from public activity.

Family Support
We go back now to that image of Oscar's mother, full of excitement, waiting for him in the airport after he had won the Nobel Prize. And that postcard makes me wonder how many of the principles Arias applies in his political life come from the family environment. He says: "The best lessons come from my parents. The principles I have had in my life

regarding responsibility, integrity, honour, intellectual honesty, the value of work, rectitude, tolerance, generosity... they all come from my parents."

Since he came to power for his second term as President of Costa Rica in 2006, Arias donates his salary. He says he does not need it, and that he learned to act that way from his family. When he was a little boy, many charity organisations would go by his house, and his parents would write a cheque every month to help them. His maternal grandfather was a very selfless man: if he was wearing a jacket or a shirt and he saw a labourer in the coffee plantation with a torn shirt, he would take off his jacket and give it to that worker. "I wanted to be that way since I was little — Arias says — and I have wanted to practise that kind of generosity with the people that have less money and more necessities than I do."

I ask him what his mother was like. He tells me she was "too kind, and too *chiniadora*", which means she was very protective. Oscar recounts: "She was excessively *chiniadora*, and she pampered me more than she should have. Largely because I suffered from asthma, and when I had an asthmatic attack, I could sometimes end up in the hospital. My father, in turn, was very demanding — that is why he made me write, read and take part in essay competitions. He really taught me to enjoy reading, and that has helped me in many ways."

His mother was the one who chose his name, Oscar. That was the name of one of her brothers, who was a medic studying in the United States and died as he was finishing his degree. But the legacy would not end there. Arias' mother wanted him to be a doctor too, in honour of his uncle. Arias says he started studying medicine to fulfil his mother's wishes, until he was able to put down in words what were his own desires. "Look, I cannot stay here dissecting frogs; I have to do what I like. I cannot keep on studying botany, or organic chemistry or biology." That is what Oscar said to his mother, and then started studying Political Science.

Oscar would call his parents by *usted* — the formal version of the first person singular *you* — as opposed to the informal *tú*. But it was not out of respect or distance. "It is just that here everyone refers to each other by *usted*," he tells me. "There are not many people that will use *tu* to refer to their parents. It is tradition."

Costa Rica: Oscar Arias

To Come Back

In 1990, Oscar Arias finished his first term as President of Costa Rica. Sixteen years later, he decided to come back and run for office again. It was a big risk, because all the prestige he had won, with his administration and the Nobel Prize, could all be affected by this new term that would take place in an absolutely different time. Why is it, then, that he decided to run for office once again? Arias says:

I resisted the idea of coming back to national politics. When I finished my term in 1990, it did not cross my mind that one day I could be back. But my party had lost two consecutive elections, and the leaders of the party were telling me: "If we lose for the third time, the party is over." That is the pattern of many mature democracies in the Western world. If a party does not manage in any way to stay in power, and loses election after election, it comes to an end. So I had a lot of pressure from those leaders. And then, to tell the truth, this was a country with no direction. My predecessor had signed the Free Trade Agreement. He had negotiated it with the United States, the rest of Central America and the Dominican Republic, and for a long time he did not present the project in Congress for approval, and when he finally did send it, it was obviously not approved. Then I got to power again, and it was still not approved. Costa Rica had relied on me once again and, since then, we have given this country a direction. Costa Rica is on the move again, because it had been paralyzed. We knew where we came from but we did not know where we were going to.

Oscar Arias mentions again that his administration allowed Costa Rica to be "open to the world". That economic opening, however, comes with the risk of losing cultural identity. How do you build a strong cultural identity in the times of globalisation? The Costa Rican President answers me: "It is not easy. As barriers fall down around the world in every field, not just culture but everything has become more heterogeneous. The important thing here is that the values that predominate are not just those of the United States and that the culture that predominates is not just, or fundamentally, the one of the United States. But I would say that it is more important to pay attention to values, because the people of the United States are more individualistic. And we, Latin Americans, do not wish to be like that."

Costa Rica: Oscar Arias

Besides the issue of identity, there are other features of Latin American reality that preoccupy Arias. He describes those features with precision: "What worries me the most about our Latin America in these times are those autocratic currents that prevail in many parts of our countries. I do not think that here we can talk about that dichotomy left and right; I think that what divides us the most is the affinity with democratic values or with the creation of increasingly autocratic political regimes. For example, I had never imagined that, right now, we could witness a coup in Honduras. Right now we should have finished the agreement between Central America and European Union, but because of the coup the negotiations were paralysed."

The conversation leads us to the commemoration that will occur this year and that unites many countries in Latin America: the 200th anniversary of their independence. Under this context of Latin American history revision, it is reasonable to think that there are still unresolved matters in Latin American democracies. Which are these matters? The President of Costa Rica analyses: "The main unresolved matter is the incapacity of our political systems to create more prosperous societies. We should feel extremely proud of what we have accomplished in many fields: art, culture, literature, sports. But we have failed in the field of social and economic growth. This twenty-first century is the century of the Asiatic, it is not the century of the Latin American."

Oscar Arias was about to leave the Presidency of Costa Rica behind for the second time. What would he do the next day? He said that he would not run out of things to do; that he already had invitations to do many things. He was thrilled to think about teaching abroad, but he would also like to dedicate some time to his hobbies. This is how he pictured his immediate future: "I would like to read what I like to read, listen to the music that I want to listen. I once told the President of Argentina, Cristina Fernández, that I enjoyed listening to Roberto Goyeneche. She asked me if I had heard the singer Adriana Varela, and as I said no, she sent me many of her records. So now I want time to listen to Adriana Varela and Goyeneche. And I want to forget about reading government papers. That would be nice."

How would this Nobel Peace Prize winner like to be remembered when his term is over? If historians had to tell, in the future, who Oscar Arias was, what would he like them to say? The President answered: "Maybe they will say that I was an honest president, brave to defend my ideas and convictions. I think that the democratic institutions of this country were strengthened during my administrations. And peace in Central America was important too."

ECUADOR: RAFAEL CORREA
THE ECONOMIST IN POLITICS

Rafael Vicente Correa Delgado was born on 6 April 1963 in Guayaquil, Ecuador. He is married and has three children. He got his Economy degree at the Catholic University of Santiago de Guayaquil in 1987. In 1991, he got his Master's Degree in the Arts of Economy at the Catholic University of Louvain, in Belgium. In 2001, he got a Ph.D. in Economy from the University of Illinois at Urbana-Champaign. He was a teacher at the Catholic University of Guayaquil and at San Francisco de Quito University. In 2005 he was appointed Minister of Economy and Finances of Ecuador. He became the Nation's President on 15 January 2007. He was re-elected for a third term with more than 50% of the vote in February 2013.

For the first time in history, Ecuador is governed by an Economist. As is the case with many current Latin American leaders, Rafael Correa became President moving through a different path than the usual one. He is not a lawyer, he did not pursue a career in a political party and he is not from the military. He is an Economist. But he is President of Ecuador — although the road he has travelled has been, at least, sinuous. He recounts:

> I had always had an inclination towards politics — ever since I was in school I would be Class President, or Student President at university. When I was in the university, I even became president of all the other private universities of Ecuador. As I was completing my degree, I got several offers to take part as a legislator, but I saw the mediocrity of our political class and thought I should better train myself first. So it happened that I turned away from politics — I turned away from that road. When I graduated, I thought I knew nothing about the reality of my country, of the reality of the indigenous people. I remember when I was studying at the Catholic University, there was an exhibition about the indigenous issue in Ecuador, and I thought: "What issue? We do not have reservations here as they do in the United States — they are exaggerating." But after a while I thought about it more and said to myself: "What am I talking about? I know nothing about this." Thus, I decided to go and work with the indigenous people and spent one year on a mission at a height of 3,600 meters above sea level. And that is still today the best

postgraduate study I have undertaken. It was there that I realised what the indigenous issue was. The issue is the misery they have to endure due to the perpetual exclusion they have suffered. So I decided to be better prepared. I won a scholarship in Belgium, and after that, I came back to work at the Academy. Then I completed another Master's Degree and the Ph.D. I knew that sooner or later I would do something. When Alfredo Palacio got to power, he called me to be his Minister of Economy, and for me, well, it was something almost natural. I knew that sooner or later I would have to do something for the country, and that opportunity appeared before me. And that is how I started to get to where I am now.

Correa's discourse is different from that of the other leaders who say "I have been preparing my whole life to be president." But, did he ever dream of becoming president? He says: "I do not have ambitions. I am an active devout Catholic and I believe that where your treasure lies, so does your heart. My treasure does not lie in power, it lies in service. But I do not fool myself. To change the country you need power, but power as an instrument of service, not as an instrument to serve yourself at the expense of others. To be honest, I dreamt of becoming President of the Republic since I was a little boy. If you ask my mother she will tell you that I would say to her, since I was seven years old, that I was going to be president. Eighty per cent of the children will say such things, but I believe I had an inclination in me towards public service and the political life."

Forty years after what that kid used to say, Correa is President of his country and he got there moving outside the structure of parties. Why did the people believe in him? How did he get to power? Correa has his own hypothesis: "I think we had the right message in the right time. People where sick and tired of the same old people and we came with our message of change. Why the great popular support? Because they see authenticity in us. We said we were going to do something and we are doing exactly what we said we would. It was not always like this. We would vote upon a project, receive a leader through the ballot box and then the President would do the complete opposite to what he had said. He would give in to the power of the International Monetary Fund. For example, in 1999, the bankers made the country go bankrupt. That is unquestionable: the biggest crisis in history was caused by the banks. Well, the people had had it with those sneaky bankers. Then along came

Ecuador: Rafael Correa

Lucio Gutiérrez with a leftist speech and with indigenous support. He won the elections and the first thing he did was to name one of the most conspicuous bankers of the country as Minister of Economy. That was a recurrent theme: treason. So, for the first time in thirty years — with the exception, probably, of Jaime Roldós — those in power come from a political project with a candidate that has stated his plans, received the votes of the Ecuadorian people because of that, and now is doing exactly what he said he was going to. Therefore, there may be people that disagree with us on every aspect but still respect us because they see we are authentic and we do not want anything for ourselves."

Rafael Correa speaks in the first person plural. He speaks in that way because he thinks that the Ecuadorians have not voted for a person, they have voted in a project, a new hope. "Of course those projects and hopes need to come to life through human beings," he reflects. "Why do they trust me? It may be because they see themselves in me. Personally, I would much rather get together with indigenous people, informal vendors and workers. It is hard for me to meet *pelucones* (rich people) and the Ecuadorian oligarchy. It is hard for me because I believe that those elites bear the greatest responsibility for the national collapse and, also, because with their ridicule, their belief in some sort of lineage, with the pedigree they flaunt, they make me laugh." But he goes back to the plural and adds: "We have demonstrated we stand by the side of the great majorities, that we are simple men, that we enjoy being around our people and, above all — as I said before — that we are authentic. With our virtues and our many defects, with our errors — deep down we are moved by good faith and we seek nothing more than the general well-being — nothing for ourselves."

Rafael Correa says that his first challenge was to recover Ecuador's sovereignty. He argues: "This is a country that has been stripped down. Its sovereignty has been destroyed. The bureaucrats of the International Monetary Fund were more in command than our people. You cannot imagine the extent to which we were handing over our country — for example, the autonomy of the Central Bank. It was autonomous from us but completely dependent on Washington — to such a degree that the IMF had its headquarters in Ecuador's Central Bank. If I would have asked for an office as Minister of Economy I would have been charged a rent. Well, the IMF had their offices for free. The handing-over levels — regarding natural resources, economic policies, the managing of the external debt, and every other aspect — were embarrassing. Recovering that sovereignty was a great challenge. Regaining sovereignty we can become owners of our own destiny, and only then can we help the poor and solve the problem of inequality."

When Correa mentions the issue of inequality, I tell him that Latin America is not the poorest continent but it is, for sure, the one with the highest inequality — and that is a problem in Ecuador too. Can the way out of inequality be seen from an economic policies point of view or is it enough with the social policies? The Ecuadorian President answers: "A good economic policy is not conceivable without a good social policy, and vice versa. Why do you think that the economic policies of the last decades in Latin America have failed categorically? Because they were in the hands of technocrats that understand nothing but numbers. Some orthodox economists were elevated to the level of priests, without them having any kind comprehensive view of the problem. This has to be in the hands of politicians who have a comprehensive view of the matter. Economy is a little part of a whole. Even these economists who destroyed it did not understand it fully, just some parts of it. I have always told them they were more like accountants rather than economists. A good economic policy is not conceivable without a good social policy — and those social policies must have social cohesion as their goal, so that we can all feel like recipients of the benefits of that economic policy. It is as simple as that."

The Student who did not Study That Much
Luis Lazo Álvarez was the Dean of La Salle School, in Guayaquil — the school that Rafael Correa attended to. Luis shows us some papers and explains us what are those documents: "It is the Graduation Certificate, where they keep copies of the birth certificate, a photograph of the student as he entered secondary school and a photograph of the student in his penultimate year." According to Álvarez — and to Correa's report card — "from the fourth year onwards, his marks started to decline. But it was obvious, he was busier taking on more social problems — he started doing community service in retirement houses and with the boy-scouts. But, it is true that he neglected some of his subjects."

Ideas and Facts
One of the greatest challenges of the governments of Latin America nowadays is the implementation of progressive and popular policies

that can be efficiently applied — because their proposals and their history demand this from them. Are these two aspects difficult to put together? Do they tend to take different paths? Rafael Correa tells us about his view on the subject: "I do not think they exclude each other. It is true there have been discourses — and it has happened to me, I am a witness — there have been people who shared our point of view completely, but when the decisive moment came, it was a total disappointment with a lack of both pragmatism and of enforceability."

Efficiency is a quality often attributed to the more liberal spaces, while the centre-left movements are accused of being impractical. Is it possible then to be pragmatic without losing sight of the popular principles? The Ecuadorian President continues his analysis: "Our principles are very clear, we make them clear; but we are also very pragmatic and very objective, and there is no contradiction in that. You can be a great idealist but have your feet set firmly on the ground. I think we have improved many efficiency levels. I could tell you, for example, about how this year (2008) we will probably make 80 per cent of budget implementation on investments of the Central Government. In previous years, it had been 30 per cent. Those are the big changes taking place in the country. We are obsessed over efficiency and seriousness. There is still a lot to do because not everything is up to the President and his Ministers. There is an obsolete bureaucracy that has no sense of urgency. There are expired structures, laws that were made to stop you from doing anything. But little by little we are overcoming those obstacles and I can say that we are a highly efficient government, at least in comparison to previous Ecuadorian governments."

Correa's description of Ecuador's current situation brings up a new issue: how should the Government behave in the face of this idea of progressive policies that are nonetheless efficient? What is the State model that Correa imagines for Ecuador? He explains: "We have given it a lot of thought and we have changed the State model of the country. It must be a State that truly represents the collective action of its society. In the past, it used to represent the actions of the dominant groups and the groups that were a constituent part of it. We have taken huge steps forward in that respect, and the definite change will come with the new Constitution. [Author's note: it was finally approved in September 2009.] We want a State that is far more efficient, with the right systems of control and the right systems of execution. A State with public companies connected to a national development plan. Before, we did not even have a development plan. For example, when I first came to power, the Executive had twenty eight institutions assigned to the Presidency. How do you manage that? Today, the Executive Power is divided into seven large sectors, coordinating Ministries without portfolio — whose only task is to coordinate, connect and carry out management control functions — and, under the control of the coordinating Ministries, there are executive Ministries. With this, I think we are gradually overcoming duplicity and overlapping. We are greatly improving efficiency."

To this series of concepts, Correa adds that in order to improve the mechanisms for social participation, a more participatory democracy is needed — one in which, for example, some levels of the budget could be designed with citizen participation. And he presents a proposal: "Maybe, as a reform of the State, we could create a fifth power — the Citizens Power — that could help to solve some contradictions with the help of citizens' representatives. For example, the authorities that control political actors are elected through the National Congress. The Prosecutor General or the Comptroller, then, get to their positions in an already biased situation, because they have to negotiate with the legislators and with the different political forces to be elected as the control authority. That will all change if the Citizen Power is the one which chooses those control authorities."

I ask him about a social agent that we have not yet talked about in depth: the indigenous communities. How can they be made to have more weight in the decision-making processes? Correa thinks, and says: "A mistake was made there: corporatism. To think that participation meant giving some directory positions to indigenous people and other positions to business men was a terrible thing to think, because they lose track of the common good and defend sectorial and group interests, no matter how legitimate or important they might be. We think it is not wholesome. We are creating a new design that will consist of directories, consulting boards, where the actors indeed will participate even if they have conflicting interests. But decision making has to be done through directories that have democratic legitimacy, that have come from a source, named by an authority and democratically elected."

A Change of Era

When analysing the current scene in Latin American, a group of policies that are common to several countries can be appreciated. Many times it has been said that we are living an era of change, but Correa would rather speak about a change of era — without making it a play on words. He explains: "In the nineties, Latin America was a disaster due to the implementation of the policies of the Washington Consensus — a consensus in which we were not even involved. Whose consensus was it? It was the consensus of the power groups, the owners of the world. And how many clowns appeared in Latin America because of that! Carlitos Menem — who took his hairdresser on his travels — Collor de Mello in Brazil, Fujimori in Peru. One can imagine the level of prostration, regarding leadership, to which Latin America fell. And what do we see in the twenty-first century? That all those sell-out governments, all those puppets, crumbled like a house of cards and progressive governments are coming with a historical vision, seeking integration and, above all, with great political capital — and highly popular. Do you know why? Because Latin American people recognise their authenticity, their true commitment to popular causes and that they are not the usual traitors. That is the change of era."

It is expressed in some analyses that this change is attributable to the favourable economic situation Latin America experiences due to the price of commodities and raw materials. For other analysts, the twist in politics has to do with the fact that the United States is no longer interested in controlling the region and has "neglected its backyard". There are those who say that change comes from the popular movement and from the maturity of societies. What does Rafael Correa think about this? He says: "I believe in the awakening of the Latin American people, but of course, there have been factors that have contributed to this. I think George W. Bush has helped a lot in waking up Latin America. His ineptitude regarding foreign policy has been such, that it awoke a great reaction that has helped progressive governments achieve a change in direction in Latin America. Regarding the idea that this favourable economic situation is a consequence of the prices of commodities... well, it is the same old story: when a government breaks the *status quo* they try to discredit its victory, its support. That is why here, everything that is not aligned with the dominant thinking is called populist. And populism has never been properly defined. We are highly popular governments, which is a different thing. Take a look at Hugo Chávez. He was President since 1998 and with great popular support. There is an awakening of the Latin American people that are finally starting to take hold of their own destinies. They feel represented by governments that have the common good in mind and are not thinking about Washington or their personal agendas — governments that are no longer speaking in Spanish and thinking in English."

In the meeting that took place in March 2008 in Brasilia — where the Constitutive Treaty of UNASUR (United Nations of South America) was signed — there was indeed some common ground shared by all the members, but it was also apparent that the particular problems between some of the countries still had their weight. There were previous conflicts between Argentina and Uruguay, between Chile and Bolivia, between Colombia and Ecuador. Could those differences affect the unity between governments? Correa analyses: "The greatest challenge is to show definite and quick results out of this integration. Our people can show their lack of acceptance towards it if it does not result in an improvement of the well-being of Latin American people. Thus, I think that this integration should address common problems and give swift answers to those problems."

I wonder if such integration is possible given the huge inequality in the inland parts of the countries and between countries themselves. Correa thinks: "It is completely possible. But we need to take those inequalities like the European Union did. There are things that, besides external and internal asymmetries, are beneficial for all of us — for example, economic integration. If we put together all our reserves, we have enough to finance ourselves and not ask for money outside the region. In the present, on the contrary, we are financing the first world — with the autonomous central banks' pandering that controls the reserves of our countries. Thus, we have great hope in that regard: the Bank of the South."

The subject takes us to another issue that has been addressed by some of the other Latin American leaders: the notion of a twenty-first century Socialism. Does that thought have an essence? Correa thinks it does, and explains his stance.

Neighbours

A bearded man who knew Correa when he was still a boy remembers:

> He used a blue uniform and wore very big glasses. To see Rafael Correa is to see the manners of a boy scout, he cares for the poor. He is one of the few who have not been changed by the Presidency

of the Republic." An elderly woman, a neighbour of Correa's family, shows us the house where Rafael lived as a boy and recounts: "As a boy he was like every other, affectionate; and he liked to investigate things as a game. He was very inquisitive. Oh! And he liked to boss his brothers around." A man from the province of Sucumbios gives his opinion of Correa: "When we see that a President comes to a province like ours, and to a city like Nueva Loja, and comes to a market, it is because he is with the people. When the others came, they would only come to the stage, guarded by a hundred or two bodyguards, then get on a plane and leave right away. In my twenty years living here, it is the first time that a president has a meal with the *chira* people, the poor people.

The essence is clear — for example, the supremacy of human labour over capital. One of the biggest victims of the long and sad night of neoliberalism was human labour. With the euphemism of "labour flexibilisation" what they did was to break our workers soul. Here, when I got to power, there were contracts that intended not to pay employment rights to the workers. For example, a toy business would employ university students for three weeks, during Christmas time, from six to ten in the evening. When I got to power, the rules established by Lucio Gutiérrez regarding the hourly contract established that you could have up to 70% of your employees signed on an hourly and permanent basis. Can you picture that? So, what is one of the characteristics of twenty-first century socialism? The ratification of the supremacy of human labour over capital. Human labour is not a means of production; it is the goal itself of that production. Human labour should not be used in favour of capital accumulation. The capital and all the other production factors should act in favour of human labour and of human beings. That is the first shared idea with classical socialism. The second one is the search for social justice — an outcry that cannot be delayed in the most unequal region in the world. It must be the solid foundation where all public policies must rest. The third shared thought is the necessity of collective action. The story that says that individualism and egoism — praised as the greatest of economic and social values — have been the motor for this world is the greatest fallacy of all. If you look thoroughly at the development processes of the countries that we currently call developed, you will find that they have always given preference to or imposed collective action in order to dominate and regulate the market and reach the desired goals. And how do you achieve this collective action? At a social level, through its institutionalised presentation: the State. And here, what was intended was to destroy everything that was public, minimise the State. Planning was destroyed. It is in all those regards that we agree with the claims of traditional socialism. But in which aspects are we different from it? In that, in the twenty-first century, the weapons are the votes and the armies are the citizens. Dialectical materialism, violent change, class struggle — they can no longer be accepted. And what other differences? That, precisely, in order to avoid those contradictions we had to get rid of private property, private companies. In the twenty-first century, who could hold such a nonsensical idea? What is intended through twenty-first century socialism is that we become an owner's society — that we democratise that asset. Another great difference? The dogmas, fundamentalisms and catechisms. Twenty-first century socialism is in constant change, under construction — socialism in progress. We know that, besides the points in common we might share, the realities of Ecuador and Venezuela, or Bolivia and Venezuela, or Bolivia and Argentina are different. And each country has to look for specific answers but knowing the question first. Those catechisms would have the answers even before knowing the question. And a fundamental difference — one of classical socialism's biggest mistakes — is that it did not differentiate itself from capitalism in its conception. What it proposed was, theoretically, a faster and fairer way of achieving development as defined by capitalism. But it was basically the same: accumulation, materialism. Now, twenty-first century socialism presents new conceptions of development, different from what classical socialism has always proposed, and different indeed from what capitalism proposes.

The Happy Utopia

We leave behind the sphere of concrete policies and ideas to enter the sphere of dreams. What is the legacy that Correa imagines he will leave after his term is over? He answers: "My dream is to leave a country without misery. We do not wish to be an opulent society. We do not measure development by 'how well are the ones who had always been well doing' but by 'how well are the ones who had never been well doing'. Our fundamental priority, our preferential option, is to decrease poverty in this country. And my dream is to leave a country with no misery, but it is hard to reach such a goal. At least, we plan to leave a country pointing irreversibly in a direction of development according to our conception — where the classes that have always ruled will not have the greatest technology and swim about in opulence, but rather the ones that had never had anything will finally be able to access a good standard of living."

Dreams. Utopias. Does happiness play an important role to reach utopias? Correa reflects: "Well, Goytisolo said: 'A utopia is something we have tried and failed to accomplish,' and we have not even got started. I think we need to dream, dream big. We do not limit ourselves to the canons, to the codes that the current models impose on us. We do not dream that Ecuador will become the Switzerland of the Andes, but rather that Switzerland will, someday, want to be the Ecuador of the Alps. That is also a part of the change of era. We dream big. But we are also very pragmatic. We aim at the social maximum. And everything we do, we must do with joy, because if we are going to do it with pain, sacrifice, lack of hope, then maybe we should all go home. We have stated that the citizen's revolution must also be a revolution of happiness — let them take away everything but not happiness."

Every morning when the President wakes up, is it happiness that prevails? He answers: "Not always. Sometimes you feel tired, stressed, worried... but it is then that I say to my closest advisors: 'Lay me down to sleep'. I am a man that works a lot, but at some point I say to myself: 'Today I am spending the day with my family', or I go to my son's choir performance. We know how to protect those spaces, I insist, so that we do not lose our joy. And that joy is not easy to keep — but when it is lost, you have to stop... and get it back." And he says this with a smile on his face.

Nicaragua: Daniel Ortega
Revolution and Death

José Daniel Ortega Saavedra was born on 11 November 1945 in the city of La Libertad, department of Chontales, Nicaragua. He is married to the poet Rosario Murillo Zambrano and has seven children. He studied law at the Central American University of Managua for a year, but dropped out to join the Sandinista National Liberation Front in 1963. In 1965 he was promoted to Commander and member of the Front's National Directorate. In 1967 he was imprisoned, and liberated in 1972. In 1974 he went to Cuba and returned to Nicaragua the next year. In 1980 he became coordinator of the Government's Junta, representing the Sandinista Front. In 1984 he was elected President of the Republic and he governed from 1985 to 1990. In 2007 he became President once again and was re-elected in 2011.

"It is difficult to be self-critical". Daniel Ortega, President of Nicaragua, makes reference to the performance of the Sandinista National Liberation Front while in power during the eighties. And he adds: "It is not easy to be self-critical regarding a revolution, because of the drive and strength that revolutions always have. They have such strength that it is very hard to go back in time and think about what would have happened if we had done this or that." But the story starts a long time before.

In the nineteen twenties, Augusto Sandino was the leader of the Nicaraguan resistance against the occupying army of the United States in Nicaragua. He was assassinated by Anastasio Somoza, head of the National Guard in 1934. Two years after the assassination of Sandino, Somoza got to power through a coup and ruled in Nicaragua for sixteen years, with a gap between 1947 and 1950. When he died, his son Luis Somoza Debayle became his successor. In 1961, Carlos Fonseca founded the Sandinista National Liberation Front to oppose, precisely, the dictatorship of Somoza Debayle.

The Nicaraguan leader started getting involved in politics short before the founding of the Front. He was thirteen years old. He recounts: "At that time, we were experiencing student struggles, and my father was the promoter. In these protests, my two brothers and I would constantly get detained. The first demonstration I attended was a protest against a massacre that had taken place in Honduras, and a movement known as Patriotic Nicaraguan Youth started to take shape, raising, once again, the flag of Augusto Sandino."

For Ortega and all the other supporters of the movement that, like him, wanted to change Nicaraguan social reality, the fight against the dictatorship was the main driving force of their political action. However, Ortega admits that his revolutionary feeling comes also from somewhere else: "It has to do with the sense of belonging I found in the family when I got to know Christ. I come from a Catholic, Christian family, but in a context of rebellion. My father was a supporter of Sandino and my mother had been detained by the dictatorship, but before I read Marx, Lenin and Engels, I met a very rebellious Christ."

Ortega was involved with the Patriotic Youth and it was there that he first encountered the consequences of the revolutionary frenzy. He says: "In the Youth we were organised in cells at first, and from these cells we started organising sabotage actions against the vehicles of the United States embassy and against the Somozist Guard. After one of those protests, I was captured — and that was the first time I went to prison. And just like that, when I was fifteen years old, I got to know what torture was. The torture room was in the Presidential House — in the basements, on one side. It was there where the political prisoners were taken to, and you knew from the moment you saw that hill, that you were heading for torture."

After that first episode, Ortega was imprisoned many times. He joined the Revolutionary Student Front, which was the student branch of the recently founded Sandinista Front. In those times, the members of the Front would go to Guatemala to train with the guerrillas of that country. As soon as they arrived, they were captured by the police and, once again, they were tortured. The Cuban revolution had already succeeded, and most of the questioning had to do with the relations these young guerrillas maintained with Cuba. Then, the police handed them to Somoza.

Ortega's life became a state of constant hiding and secrecy. Only twenty years old, he was promoted to Commander and member of the National Directory of the Sandinista National Liberation Front, along with Carlos Fonseca. He organised the Popular Civic Committees and a web of urban guerrillas. In 1967, Ortega was arrested again, and this time it meant seven years in prison. Nicaragua's President remembers that moment with precision: "I was imprisoned from November 1967 to December 1974. There were 120 cells and we — seven prisoners — were separated, completely isolated. I remember there was a sign that said: "No speaking. No singing. No smoking. No sitting. No talking to the guards." Those were the orders during the day. And during the night, the lights would remain on, so that the guards could see us. And so, we had to go through long hunger strikes — one, for example, lasted almost forty days. Anyways, with the help of some guards we started developing a web to communicate with our comrades. We would give them messages to deliver; they would get books or the newspaper for us. The truth is that, as time went by, I grew accustomed to that life."

I ask him if he ever thought, during those seven years, that the struggle was meaningless, or that the movement was not going to be successful. Ortega says: "No, we always thought of prison as another combat trench. And the experience forged us — it strengthened us. Prison was a challenge and we had the certainty that we would get out at some point or another. We made many escape plans, but they always found out about them. Then there was one escape attempt that almost got us all killed. Actually, it had been organised by infiltrators that worked for Somoza. They were waiting for us to escape so they could kill us, and we were saved by some comrades that warned us just in time."

The release of Ortega and his comrades took place thanks to Archbishop Obando, who was one of the few people who could break the isolation and visit the prisoners.

Ortega in the Spotlight

People from different fields of Nicaraguan society give their opinion of Daniel Ortega. A journalist from El Nuevo Diario says: "As a human being, Daniel Ortega is an enigma. People became disenchanted with the right-wing governments that had not solved the most profound problems of our society, and so, they saw change in Daniel Ortega. If it is not Ortega, then no one can govern Nicaragua right now." A man sitting on his metal chair in Managua says: "Ortega is a committed and hardworking man that has an aura of mystique. A man that wants consensus and that keeps his promises." Another Nicaraguan man adjusts his green shirt and then gives his opinion: "More than a President, Daniel Ortega is a political agitator. Many people love him or hate him, but it is difficult to be indifferent towards him. I would say that Nicaraguan history would be incomplete without Daniel Ortega." Another person defines Ortega as a preacher, another one says that he is a big interrogation mark and a young boy points out: "Ortega is one of those men that are born once every one hundred years."

The story Daniel Ortega tells me makes me think about the relationship a guerrilla man has with death. What is that relationship like? Ortega reflects: "One starts preparing for the greatest risks, including death. And, half-jokingly, we would say: 'Let's see when your turn comes'; because, of course, comrades died constantly. I was close to death many times — at the demonstrations, in prison or in combat where bullets flew all over you."

Sandino and Fonseca

Daniel Ortega is one of Nicaragua's most important revolutionary leaders, along with his predecessors Augusto Sandino and Carlos Fonseca. How did he first encounter the figure of Sandino? Ortega recounts: "My first approach was through my father, because he supported Sandino and kept letters they had exchanged. That is to say, that first approach came through the legend, the conversations, and not through reading, because at that time there were no Sandino books yet in Nicaragua apart from the one issued by Somoza. Once in the Patriotic Youth, we started forming study groups and got to know more about Sandino. At that time, from Cuba and clandestinely, entered the first edition of the book *Sandino, general de hombres libres* (*Sandino, General of Free Men*) by Gregorio Selser. It had been published, originally, in Argentina. That book was gold here. We were all looking for that book."

The first news from Fonseca came when Ortega was already active in the Sandinista Front and Fonseca got wounded in combat at the Chaparral zone. The President of Nicaragua recounts it like this: "I met Carlos personally in prison. He was captured after the first guerrilla incursion in the cities of Bocay and Raití. There, he wrote a pamphlet he titled "From Prison I Accuse the Dictatorship". It was the first of Carlos' writings I held in my hands and that we clandestinely distributed around the cities. Then, the first real encounter I had with Carlos was in Pancasán, when he joined the guerrilla. This is the year 1967."

Daniel Ortega tells me that he started having a very close relationship with Carlos Fonseca. Fonseca went to the mountains and Ortega stayed in charge of the resistance in Managua — but he would travel permanently to have meetings and decide the next steps. It was already clear that they were fellow travellers in this journey, and they both had responsibilities in the command of the Front. Fonseca was the one who insisted that the movement should incorporate Sandino's legacy into its references. Ortega gives more details: "Carlos suggested we incorporate the Sandinista movement because he thought those were our values, our history. It caused some controversy, but in the end, the National Liberation Front became the *Sandinista* National Liberation Front."

The Guerrilla Comes to Power

Ortega's case is one of a kind in Latin America: He was a guerrilla man that took part in the armed struggle against an authoritarian regime; a man that managed to get to power and who shortly after was elected President through the ballot.

In 1979, Anastasio Somoza Debayle, son of the first dictator and Luis' brother, was overthrown by the Sandinista Front. The government was now in the hands of the Junta of National Reconstruction that was created in the face of the imminent fall of the Somoza dictatorship. A transitional system was established and the Junta was recognised as the government of the country. At this time, Ortega was in Costa Rica. When he got back to Nicaragua, the Front took control of the Junta and he became the coordinator of that government body. As a matter of fact, Ortega was the President of the Republic. In November 1984 he called for elections which he won by 63 per cent of the votes. In January 1985 he legally started his presidency.

Had the revolutionary Daniel Ortega imagined he could become President of Nicaragua? He says: "The truth is that we had the conviction that the revolution would succeed, but we also had the conviction that we would die in combat, that we were not going to be alive to see the moment of victory. We went into war with that in mind. That is to say, 'we will not be able to see it, but victory will be ours'. If we did not even imagine ourselves living long enough to see us be victorious, let alone that we would live through this long period. I could say, like that song goes: 'thanks to life, that has given me so much'. The most touching moment was when I saw, for the first time, the image of Sandino on television, taking his hat off and waving. The Front had taken control of the television channel. It was something that made me cry. Seeing that, I realised that we had won."

The revolutionaries had come to power. The question is: were they ready to govern? Ortega analyses: "We had prepared a model of government that had to do with the passing from a traditional guerrilla to an insurrectional guerrilla that would get the people involved in the struggle. The people were merely observers at that time, so we decided to go for an insurrectional strategy. We said: "We can no longer stay trapped in the jungle. We need to go to the cities — to where the people is." We thought that we needed a very wide front that would look for ways, through a programme, of bringing the higher sectors of the population and economic strata and the anti-Somozists closer. We had to take hold of the quarters in the different regions, towns, departments. Give the people a minimum of preparation so that when the quarters came down, the people would know they had to fight and not wait for the guerrilla. And right then we started developing a government programme, gathering people of different sectors that would agree with our vision. That is how Violeta Chamorro, Sergio Ramírez, Moisés Hassan and Alfonso Robelo joined in. They all had their own characteristics. When we were close to victory, we already had a government plan accepted by these people I have just mentioned — it was accepted by different sectors."

The question is, then, could the government plan of the Sandinista Front accomplish the transformations it wished to accomplish? Daniel Ortega says that the economic structures that had previously existed were all eradicated, and that the military structure was modified. He adds: "A new military power was established based on the ideas of the revolution, the ideas of the people. Great changes were made in the economic field, in the field of property, and that caused enormous contradictions. And in 1984 we had elections; that was a way of legitimising the revolution in the face of the Yankee aggression. It was also the time to write a Constitution, because the country had none up to then — it had only a provisional charter. The National Assembly was established, and it was in session from 1985 to 1987. In January 1987, the new Nicaraguan Constitution was published. Its fundaments were: multi-party system, mixed economy and non-alignment to empire."

What do the Sandinistas mean when they talk about a mixed economy? Ortega explains: "It meant that there should be the most varied forms of property — collective property, State property, associative property, individual property, small, medium, large; that there could be no *latifundia* or idle land; that the strategic areas for the economy, regarding businesses and basic services, had to be in the hands of the State. All of these were the elements of a mixed economy, with which we managed to boost the agro-industrial sector. We managed to create, amid war, conditions that had never existed in our country — that capitalism had been unable to create in Nicaragua. The heart of this mixed economy was an economy where all the different forms of association — family and individual economy too — could move around."

More than twenty years after the coming to power of the Sandinista movement, it could be said, with some perspective, that the period that ended in 1990 meant great conflict and many changes. I ask the President of Nicaragua which were the negative elements — from his point of view — of that process. But then, Ortega tells me again about how difficult it is to be self-critical when talking about a revolutionary process. Nonetheless, he gives his analysis of the situation:

The Opposite Side of the Street

The Sandinista Renovation Movement (Movimiento Renovador Sandinista or MRS, in Spanish) is a Nicaraguan political party that was formed in 1995 due to differences between members of the Sandinista National Liberation Front. One of its founders was Sergio Ramírez Mercado, who had been Vice President during Ortega's first term. In a demonstration of the MRS, historic leader Dora María Téllez said:

> Ortega is proving to be completely incapable of governing the country and the only thing he is doing is to close down democratic spaces. If he wants to eliminate the rights of the Nicaraguan people, then he has to go."

> I think that the crucial element was the historical contradiction that has existed between the United States' imperialism and Nicaragua. Why? Due to our geopolitical location and the transit route. That has been the reason for imperial domination over Nicaragua, that it was a reserve for the Panama Channel. Thus, when the United States discovers that we are establishing a revolutionary, solidary, anti-imperialist regime here, war follows almost immediately. At that time, I visited the United States, where I met Jimmy Carter at a United Nations event. Carter told me: "Now you have to change," to which I answered: "No. It is you who have to change". Right there I told him that Nicaragua needed to build a new army — weapons, and this and that. His answer was "no weapons". So we started looking for weapons elsewhere and an envoy from the United States came to me and asked me why we were arming

ourselves. He told me that they did not accept that we arm ourselves, especially with weapons that came from socialist sectors, because they saw it as a threat to their security. I told him that we needed to protect our citizens from them and he told me: "Haven't you realised that the United States has to do as much as lifting a finger and it will crush you like a cockroach? Those weapons will do you no good." In that context we could discuss mistakes, but, how far? How can we talk about mistakes in such violent and unsettled conditions? And, after all, what weights is the decision of defending a process. Of course we say: "Why weren't we more flexible with the right-wing position in the Government Junta?" But, then, what we would have done would have been to accept Somozism without Somoza. If we had accepted Somozism without Somoza, they would have called us "democrats" — the United States would have immediately praised us; then all the right-wing governments would have praised us; then the whole capital; immediately, all the right-wing media. But our path was another, and the reason for our struggle was to make a revolutionary change. As far as mistakes go, it could be argued that we did not hurry enough to make the agrarian reform — that we placed greater emphasis on strengthening the State businesses instead. It could be argued that we did not manage our disagreements with the Church correctly in a country that is so Christian and faithful. We could talk about a series of elements and effectively call them mistakes — but due to the phenomenon's magnitude, to talk about cause and effect really escapes these elements that are manifested as a result of such a violent breakup.

There is another critique to Ortega's government, from a traditional left-wing point of view, regarding the fact that it called for elections in 1990. That year, Violeta Chamorro won over Daniel Ortega after distancing herself from the movement that had reached power. Ortega says that it had been already established by a constitutional rule that there would be elections in Nicaragua every six years. "And there was a majority that decided to vote for the right-wing government in 1990 — he laments — but there is nothing to do but to respect that. And we handed over the power; but we are still ready to defend the achievements of the revolution."

Nicaragua: Daniel Ortega

A Return

On 10 January 2007 Daniel Ortega returned to power as President of Nicaragua, after winning the elections with ten points over his competitor, Eduardo Montealegre. The international circumstances are not the same as when the Front made the revolution. Which moment is more favourable for the Sandinista movement? Ortega analyses: "The fact that we are coming to power through the ballots amid these new circumstances for Latin America gives us tools we did not previously have — tools that could even neutralise the empire's aggressions. There have been extraordinary and profound changes in Latin America. We are facing a new stage, with Latin American identity, with banners, with the spirit of unity, of integration."

In his new term, Ortega has given priority to public health, education and a programme of zero hunger. Are there international conditions that favour these kinds of transformations? The Nicaraguan President says: "I would say that the international conditions had always been against us. As long as capitalism is out there imposing its tyranny, headed by the United States, we have an element that conspires against any programme. It is that model that has the world in these conditions. What is it that will bring about or is bringing about new spaces that open up despite the model? Well, working to integrate, to unite, to open our own spaces with a proposal of solidarity, with a proposal of complementarity, with a proposal of fair trade. But we are in better conditions now that before, because now we have the chance to unite and consolidate those spaces. In the past we did not. In the past, it was each country for itself, subject to the dictates and laws of empire — the laws of global capitalism."

Thirty years after the Sandinista revolution, the Nicaraguan people are still very poor. Democracy, over the past years, could not put an end to this state, but Nicaraguan society still believes in democracy. Ortega says that his countrymen had gone for conservative governments since 1990 out of a survival instinct, because they were told that "if the Front comes back, the war comes back". The President adds: "Now that we have arrived in power again and the right-wing lies fall apart, where is the war? As far as we are concerned, we are busy developing plans to take people out of extreme poverty. We are being successful. Why? Because we are taking care of problems that were not a concern for previous governments — for example, the energy issue. The only thing neoliberalism did was to aggravate the energy crisis by privatising

Nicaragua: Daniel Ortega

distribution."

Venezuelan President Hugo Chávez and his peer in Bolivia, Evo Morales, called their projects "twenty-first century socialism". Is socialism possible in Latin America? In order to answer, Ortega looks for concepts that go back to the so called real socialism and from there he builds a bridge to the present time: "Socialism is an alternative that humanity has for getting to justice, peace and a real democracy. When I say socialism, I mean the kind of socialism that we knew from the Soviet Union, from the German Democratic Republic and all those countries. Those people really were caring people and governments that practised fair trade and, in commercial relations, they practised the recognition of asymmetries. I could not possibly understand the consolidation of the Cuban revolution or the Sandinista revolution without the existence of the socialist field. Who can doubt the kindness of the Soviet Union towards the people of the south? There has been no capitalist country that has behaved that way towards a country of the south. I think that in these new circumstances we cannot forget all the good things we have inherited from those times, from the first expressions of socialism in the world. And if we take that essence and enrich it, correct it and direct it through the historical processes that each country in Latin America lives, I think that the necessary elements to take us to socialism are there. In order to get there we need to break up from the hegemonic policies. We need to strengthen the Latin American, African and Asian spaces."

Nicaragua has changed since the victory of the Sandinista revolution. Latin America has changed — the world too. But, how has Daniel Ortega changed since the times of that guerrilla man that in 1979 leaded the first Government Junta to the current Daniel Ortega, President of Nicaragua? He says: "First of all, I am some years older, but even my enemies say it, I have not changed much. I can wear a shirt of a certain colour and later use a shirt of some other colour, but that is as much as I change. I cannot change my principles. What needs to change is the world. For us to stop talking about imperialism there has to be no more imperialism. They tell me my discourse is repetitive, but I always say the same because the story is always the same."

Paraguay: Fernando Lugo
A Priest with a Presidential Sash

Fernando Armindo Lugo Méndez was born on 30 May 1951 in the locality of San Solano, in the San Pedro de Panamá district, Itapúa department, Paraguay. In 1969, he completed his studies at the Regional Centre of Education in Encarnación and that enabled him to exercise as a school teacher. In 1972, he graduated in Science of Religion at the Catholic University Nuestra Señora de la Asunción. In 1977, he was ordained a priest. Between 1983 and 1987 he studied Sociology with a specialisation in Social Doctrine of the Church at the Pontifical Gregorian University of Rome. In 1994, he was ordained bishop and was assigned the diocese of San Pedro. In 2005, he resigned as a bishop and, in 2006, he sent his resignation from the priesthood to the Vatican so he could dedicate himself to political activity. However, the institution did not accept his resignation and suspended him from his charge a divinis. In April 2008 he won the Presidential elections, and from August of that same year he governed Paraguay. In June 2012, Lugo was impeached and removed from office by the Congress of Paraguay, in a "parliamentary coup".

How do you imagine the last day of your term as President?

I imagine myself in an oasis of peace. Maybe I will turn to writing. I will continue to pray a lot. Probably, if everything goes right — and I hope it will — I will take a deep breath, satisfied because I have served the motherland. If I leave a different country for my successor, maybe I will sleep in peace that night.

And which would be the personal distinguishing feature that you would like people to remember about your administration?

The humbleness. I do not consider myself an intellectual, nor above the rest of the people. I see myself as a road companion for the Paraguayans that want and dream of a different country. I would like to be remembered as someone who was generously devoted to the people. Maybe, as a President that tried, by all means, to inspire genuine democracy for his country — which he loves so much — and that recovered the dignity and the sovereignty of the country. Maybe it is too presumptuous for me to think I will be remembered like that.

Paraguay: Fernando Lugo

This conversation with Fernando Lugo, President of Paraguay, took place before he took office. So, at that time, his administration was all hope, all future time, and the expectations ran high because Lugo was about to become the first ex-bishop ever to take office as President of a Latin American country. What extra responsibility did being a religious man carry? Lugo said: "I know that being President is different from the pastoral action that I have carried out for thirty years. I think this is bigger and more complicated — without any intention to discredit the episcopal exercise. I think that the country is at stake in this field — as well as a trajectory, a testimony. I think that the political process in Paraguay will be a truly inside process — a process from the people, from the bottom up, where the citizens' participation will differentiate this regime from previous ones."

Lugo also speaks about the responsibility that lies in ending with sixty one years of the Colorado Party hegemony in power and the hope of elaborating a new political paradigm. For Lugo, in this new era, there are other things at stake: "Governability, the development of the people and the chance to push the country forward — a country that is isolated, has a huge poverty rate and is landlocked not only geographically but also at a commercial and cultural level."

But, how did the political vocation emerge from someone who has been a teacher and a priest? When did the possibility of becoming president come up? Fernando Lugo says: "People talked. Even when I started as a bishop, some journalist already thought that I could be president. I was an atypical bishop, because I spent time with the people and would only go once a week to the Episcopal Palace. A natural leadership arose in the region — a religious leadership with strong social ingredients."

His political story was rapidly written. Lugo left San Pedro city in 2005 and headed towards Encarnación, where he had planned to teach in a rural Church. But he was offered to be headmaster at a school in Asunción, and he accepted. At the capital city, where many things that concern the country are decided, he met different social groups of artists, farmers, workers, unionists and politicians. That is how the initiative to create the Citizen's Resistance organisation was born. Later, the National Concentration (*Concentración Nacional*) was formed and from the National Concentration, the Patriotic Alliance for Change was formed. On 7 December 2006, Lugo was presented over 100,000 signatures from farmers, workers and local communities asking him to make the sacrifice of resigning his episcopal pastoral exercise and turn to politics to lead a big coalition. "That night was the longest night of my life — says Lugo — and I could not sleep. It was the night of the great choice."

A House with History

Mercedes Lugo Maidana, Fernando Lugo's sister, shows us the house where their family has always lived and she tells us: "At this gate was where Fernando announced he was resigning his diocese. It was from here that we started our long march the day he took office." Mercedes enters the house and presents a room: "This was the room where all the brothers would eat. In this room we also had a wake for one of our brothers who died in an accident." Then, Mercedes steps out into a patio and describes: "Here is where we were sitting when Fernando said: 'What would you say if I go into the political arena?'"

Given his actual position, one can guess his decision. But that determination was consulted and discussed many times. He recounts: "I talked it over with some people very close to me. My spiritual director, some priest friend, someone close from the Society of the Divine Word. Once the decision was taken, we had over six hundred meetings across the country, where we gave not even one speech, because we simply listened to what the people had to say. This has enriched us very much — it has given us a distinctive signature as to what making politics means: listening to the people."

I ask him if being a good listener is a fundamental feature of him as a political leader. "I think it is. Here, the politician is the one who talks a lot, the one with the magic formula, the one who always talks, the one who does well in his last speech. And I am not used to that," Lugo answers.

The political history of the Lugo family dates a long way back before Fernando became President. His parents were imprisoned during Alfredo Stroessner's dictatorship, and many of his brothers had to go into exile. In some way, it seems there has been a family legacy in the current President of Paraguay's political search. Lugo describes it:

In 1962 I was in the sixth grade, my father was in prison, and after ten month of so much torture he came out almost blind. I will never forget that day. He came home and his strength cheered us all up. It was an encounter I can never forget — it is stuck forever in my memory. There is another anecdote from that time: One day, very early in the morning, the police came, broke into the house and took my father. He disappeared for five months. We had no idea where he was. After five months we heard he was in a prison in Asunción — a closed prison where he could not see the sunlight. And all those things made me react: this cannot happen again, ever. Persecution, torture, unfair imprisonment — never again for a country that needs to live in democracy, in freedom.

Then he tells me that one of his brothers used to say that once the "virus of politics" gets into you, that vocation will surface at some time or another. However, when Fernando was young, he chose the religious path, not the political. How did he come to take that road? In his own words: "I was young and I went to the countryside to teach. I was one of the best graduates of my class but, as I was not a member of the Colorado Party, they sent me to the countryside, almost to the forest. When I was there, I started reading the Bible. I carried an almost unconscious, ritualistic Christianity in me, but then I started reading and I found the real impoverished Christ in the people, in the kids who were barefooted in the cold, in the kids for whom we made breakfast, in the fathers that worked the land from dawn to dusk and could not provide well-being to their families. I think that it was there that I found myself — away from home for the first time, in a different environment, in the countryside. That left a mark in me. It was my decision to work for others — all my strength, my determination, my intelligence and my heart were at the service of the neighbour."

During the seventies, a religious movement asked the question of how to be a Christian in an oppressed continent like America. That movement was called Liberation Theology. "How can we manage to make our faith liberating instead of alienating?" was another of the questions that the movement recited. Fernando Lugo was ordained priest in 1977, and until that moment, he had heard nothing about the Liberation Theology. But Lugo travelled to Ecuador, to continue with his pastoral activities, and there he found out about it. "I was shocked by the gap between the wealthy, rich people and the poor people throughout history. And I met Leonidas Proaño, the indigenous bishop — 'the bishop with the striped poncho', as they would call him. We have shared long conversations, retreats, meetings, discussions. Up to that time, I would associate priesthood only with religious and spiritual tasks. But in Ecuador I learnt another way of exercising priesthood. Faith cannot be disembodied, alien to the social and cultural matters," recounts the Paraguayan President.

Proaño was the bishop who took on the task, radically, of evangelizing the culture of the native people. He was a major influence on Fernando Lugo. "I was impressed by his simplicity, his humbleness, the words he used. He was not pretentious, and his words, his gestures, his life… it was all in favour of getting his message through at all costs," remembers Lugo.

The Happy Little Priest

Father Justino Torres works at the San Roque González de la Santa Cruz Church where Fernando Lugo was ordained a priest. Justino has his own opinion about Lugo's resignation to his religious vows: "I am sure he resigned such a beloved vocation like priesthood because he saw how the people in his country were suffering. We all expected a lot from him — and now even more. He knows his people very well, he knows the processes he has to carry out, and we all hope this Paraguay will truly change with him." Marcos Pereira Florentín, a priest at San Pedro Apóstol Cathedral says: "At San Pedro, if there is something special that identifies or characterises Lugo that we want to see, it is his committed support to the popular recognition movements of all sorts. By his side, there are no worries, everything is joy."

Changing

It could be said that Fernando Lugo was a rebel both as a teacher and as a priest. Could it be that he would also be a rebellious President? What would that name mean to him? "To be rebellious as President you have to break the mould, and I will refer again to Jesus of Nazareth for this: he broke with all pre-established moulds — he did not even respect the Sabbath law. He was against laws that enslave," Lugo analyses.

To break the mould, for Lugo, could also mean not to let down those who have put their trust in him. He expresses his feelings through an anecdote: "When I became a priest, my friends back in my neighbourhood told me: 'We ask you one thing only. Do not change'. They asked me to remain the way I was — honest, open, simple. Those same people told me the same thing when I became a bishop. And now they say to me: 'Now that you are President, we cannot talk to you, you cannot play a volley match with us, or have a roasted meat or drink like we used to'. For me, 'do not change' has great meaning — it means to be the child, the young man, the teenager, the grown up that keeps in touch with the citizens, with no prejudice."

Facing such expectations, the risk is to feel afraid of the responsibilities that lie ahead. He then admits to feel such fear and says that he believes that the task is to build the road day by day. "There are no diagrams, no formulas — the challenge here lies in creativity, in the relationship between parties, between the executive power and the Parliament." A few weeks before he took office, Lugo had received over four thousand requests for hearings as a sign of the great interest that his coming to power aroused.

Now we get to this point and the questions move towards the specific field of the work his government will have to do. Poverty, problems regarding education and the agrarian reform are the issues that concern Lugo the most. He explains his ideas:

Regarding poverty, let us differentiate the pastoral exercise and political exercise. Through the pastoral exercise it is possible to help the poor with solidarity. In the political arena, it is our duty to end poverty — we have to end it together: they have to be protagonists, key players. And I think we have the necessary political tools. We have the institutions and the Government. I think it is a task that requires political, social and economic engineering. One very important job we will have will be to give opportunities to everyone — to be President of all Paraguayans alike, no exclusion, no distinction. That will be a side of this Government that will be different from any previous one.

With regards to education, here, in the nineties a big educational reform started, but it has not been a genuine Paraguayan processes. We have imported it and reduced it to an urban process. That means it has not gotten everywhere in the country. Although it is true that it has expanded, it has lost quality. We have a high proportion of what we call "functional illiterates". In Paraguay, people go to school and know how to count, barely read and draw their own signature. But reading a book and understanding it are two different things. That is why we want a literacy system that promotes freedom of consciousness — that leads to a maturity of the systems of thought of each citizen. To help in the preparation of more capable and upstanding citizens that can help in the transformation and in the change the country needs.

And regarding the agrarian reform, I think that there has never been a serious comprehensive reform in this country. There are many people without a land and without a roof, and the model for the agrarian reform has to help, at the very least, the great dispossessed majorities of our country. Anyways, my model will be agro-industrial. Paraguay is the only country in the region that has a surplus of energy. We have the land and the climatic conditions to be a great producer of food. I believe that if we are able to develop these two central ideas — produce high quality foods and use our own energy in the agro-industrial process — the country can escape this situation that has limited us historically.

In Paraguay, after six decades of the same ruling party, people relate the Government not only to that particular party — the Colorado Party — but specially to corruption. Lugo's administration has, then, among its assignments, to recover the State's role. What opinion does the President of Paraguay have with respect to this topic that is central today in Latin American agendas? "The Government has to be at the service of all the Paraguayan. That will be the grand design, our great commitment. Over decades, in order to get a job you had to be affiliated to the Colorado Party — we have to overcome that. We have to give positions — public positions mainly — to people who are more capable, more honest, more transparent and more efficient," says Lugo.

The Door to Latin America
The work towards integration in Latin America is the biggest common ground shared by the majority of the current leaders of the region. Many of them remark that it is a unique movement in the history of the continent, where you can find more things in common than differences. However, inequality too is still a common ground for many of the region's countries. What is his opinion with regards to this aspect? "I think we all look forward to an integrated Latin America, both nationally and internationally. An America that has a voice of its own, that can say to the other continents: 'Here we stand, on the basis of equality.' A Latin America that can break cultural, geographical and ideological frontiers to seek real integration," he says.

I mention to him that the so called progressive sectors that govern a great part of the countries of Latin America are better known for their power of criticism than for their power of designing proposals — a great capacity for pointing out what is wrong rather than the technical capacity to transform things. What is the challenge in this sense? The President of Paraguay gives his opinion: "The Commanders-in-Chief of Latin America have the great responsibility of recovering the humanity in politics. The neoliberalist process of diminishing the State is over. In the present, we want a State model that presents a solidary and corrective Government — a State that has weight and presence in the national territory."

Paraguay is a member of Mercosur (Southern Common Market), and its asymmetries with Argentina and Brazil are evident. Lugo gives his opinion on this matter: "The good thing is that this asymmetry is recognised by the other countries. I think there is this idea that the smaller countries of Mercosur, like Paraguay or Uruguay, should have more opportunities for a more equalitarian development. Mercosur is very important for us. We are interested in taking it forward and make it not only a commercial bloc, but also a social one — a bloc of integration of our people — and a political and cultural one. It is not possible to speak of change without speaking of cultural change. In this regard, I think there are signs of hope and excitement."

The relationship between Paraguay and Argentina is a peculiar one. Between 1864 and 1870, the War of the Triple Alliance devastated the Guaraní country. For this occasion, Brazil, Argentina and Uruguay joined forces to fight Paraguay. As a result, Argentina kept territories that, up to that moment, had been Paraguayan — like that corresponding to the current Argentinian province of Chaco. But above all, that war cost Paraguay half its population.

In the twenty-first century, the situation is different. According to a 2001 census, 325,000 Paraguayans live in Argentina. However, nowadays the total amount could be around 500,000 because many of them were undocumented immigrants and we have to add the years that had passed since that census. Lugo's stance in this regard is of complete gratitude: "We have a great debt towards Argentina. It was like a second home, a second Paraguay, the second family for so many Paraguayans exiled for political or economic reasons or for the search of work, health care and education. We also thank President Cristina Fernández who has allowed the documentation of over 300,000 Paraguayans. Many Paraguayans have found comfort in Argentina and have rebuilt their lives. And we have overcome that historical confrontation to become now, above all, brother countries."

Everything is About to Get Started

Now, Fernando Lugo is back to being that ex-priest that has won the elections and that in ten days will be taking office as President of Paraguay. How does he imagine that day? What are his expectations for 5 August 2008? "On 5 August it will feel like a festivity, for us, for our family and for me specially, because it is an emblematic day. My parents got married on 5 August. On 5 August, I was ordained priest back in 1977. And even more, it is the day of the Our Lady of the Assumption. And now, on 5 August, I will take office as President of the Republic," Lugo answers.

I propose that we think about his first steps as President, his first actions. Lugo imagines: "At a personal level, I would like for not even one photograph of myself to appear in any public institution. And I honestly say that. I am against any personality or personal worship. Regarding the administration, the first steps will be a hands-on approach against corruption — formal reports, transparency. And I have asked five things to those who will be Ministers of the Executive Power: honesty, austerity, transparency, patriotism and efficiency.

Other topics arise. Lugo speaks about giving back their dignity to the indigenous people of Paraguay, about establishing the grounds for a genuine participative democracy, with equal opportunities for every Paraguayan.

Fernando Lugo is President of Paraguay. Everything is about to get started.

Uruguay: Tabaré Vázquez
The Child and the Doctor

Tabaré Ramón Vázquez Rosas was born on 7 January 1940 at the Benito Riquet neighbourhood in La Teja, Montevideo, Uruguay. He was the fourth of five brothers. He married María Auxiliadora Delgado in 1964 and they had three children. They also have an adopted son who currently lives in Venezuela. Vázquez graduated as a Doctor in 1969 and in 1976 he received a scholarship from the French government to further his studies at the Gustave Roussy Institute in Paris. In 1986 he was appointed Professor in charge of the Radiotherapy area of the Oncology Department of the Medical School at the University of the Republic and he started his own clinic. Partnered up with his colleagues Álvaro Luongo and Miguel Torres, he bought 75 per cent of the Barcia Clinic and renamed it Oncology and Radiotherapy Centre. In 1987 he joined the Uruguayan Socialist Party Central Committee and in 1989 he was elected Mayor of Montevideo. He was President of Uruguay from March 2005 to March 2010. In 2015, he was re-elected and his term will end in 2020.

The five year old kid has whooping coughs, and his parents react as is customary in Uruguay — they call the family doctor, who had already looked after his grandparents. The doctor — bold, big — rests his head on the kid's chest. He then washes his hand in a flagstone washbowl that is reserved only for these occasions and then dries them with a white embroidered towel, also reserved for these types of visits. Then he advices the family to take the kid outside to get some air near the eucalyptus. The kid, sixty years later, says that seeing the doctor arrive was enough to make him feel cured — he even remembers the perfume the doctor was wearing on that day.

That kid was Tabaré Vázquez, who was forever marked by that experience and had always had the vocation to be a doctor. The story continues: "Time went by, and when I was around twelve years old I used to hang with a group of friends in the corners of the neighbourhood, like in any neighbourhood in Montevideo, and one morning we found out that one of our friends had died. He had a very contagious tubercular lung illness and a few days after that, I started having cough symptoms. My parents were scared to death and they immediately called that same doctor. He came, checked on me, and told me it was just a momentary respiratory affection. I smelled that bold man's perfume again and my admiration was so that right then I decided I wanted to be a doctor for the rest of my life."

So, it never occurred to the man who governed Uruguay for the last five years, not even remotely, that he could become President of the Nation. Tabaré puts it clearer: "It was never my idea — not through childhood, adolescence or adult life. Because my vocation has always been and still is medicine. I prepared myself to be a doctor; I wholeheartedly prepared myself to fight a pathology like cancer. I dedicated myself to that. I went to the university — I even got to be Professor of Oncology at our country's Medicine School. I never imagined I would play any role in politics. It really came up spontaneously, as a collateral thing, and well... here we are." And here he is.

During the forties, at the time Vázquez suffered his whooping cough, the Uruguayan health care system was divided into two modalities. Some citizens could pay a mutual fee at medical companies, or they could have a general practitioner. In most cases, that practitioner lived in the neighbourhood, and he charged very little for each visit — it was in the context of the poorer regions. In one of these regions, the working class neighbourhood of Benito Riquet in La teja, Montevideo, is where little Tabaré grew up. He remembers it fondly: "I was born in a working class neighbourhood, in a humble home, in what is known here as a tin hut. They had sheet metal walls with stones on top so that when the famous south or southeast *pampero* winds or the *sudestada* wind came, the house would be protected. It was a waste ground region in the south of Montevideo."

Vázquez's childhood went by in a poverty stricken environment that, according to him, is very different from the current. "Now — Tabaré says — poverty is very marginal in some sectors. Back then, if a wealthy citizen passed by those neighbourhoods and saw us playing football with a cloth ball, with our rolled up trousers and sandals, they had no right to imagine that those kids could not become managers at banks, university professionals, Mayor or President of the Republic. We had those opportunities. Nowadays, if you pass by those marginal neighbourhoods, unfortunately, it is very difficult to see those kids become university students or have access to public positions like those we could enjoy back in those days."

Besides the material shortage, Tabaré remembers his childhood as a very joyful time. He dedicated many of those years to football — he played in the lower divisions of *Club Atlético Progreso*. He was a skilled goalkeeper and years later he came to be President of the team and President of the *Liga Universitaria de Deportes* (University Sports League). He also used to play, in his childhood, in a Salesian school of his neighbourhood. The headmaster at that school used to pick up Tabaré and his brother himself to take them to the matches. The Vázquez could not go out on their own because their father, Héctor, was a union leader in hiding. His fear was that his children would be detained and he would have to go to the police station to take them out. The kids would play and have fun, and afterwards, the priest would take them home.

Tabaré recounts: "Sometimes, my father would come to visit us early in the morning and he would come through the backyard because we had a private police guard in the corner of our house waiting for my father to come so he could take him in. And one of those mornings it happened. The police saw him and took him away. I was twelve years old, and those things leave a mark."

But Tabaré did not grow up surrounded only by gloves and football. He started working at a very early age. He sold newspapers in the buses, he did small jobs in construction, he worked at a carpenter's shop and, when he was nineteen, he started working at a wholesale shop. He worked there many years and he even had to quit his career at times because of his working schedule. After getting his degree he continued his work in the company to pay his daily expenditures.

Tabaré Vázquez attended La Teja's public school; then *Liceo del Cerro* high school in a neighbourhood nearby, and later the University of the Republic, which was also State-owned. The now ex-Uruguayan President is proud of his origins, and also thankful: "I thank my parents that made great efforts to give me and my brother the opportunity to study, but I also thank all the humble workers that paid their taxes so that we could study for free. Since I got my degree I have always prioritised social work as a way of giving back to the Uruguayan community what it had given me."

Brothers

During the military dictatorship, Jorge Vázquez, Tabaré's brother, spent thirteen years in prison. Jorge recounts: "I was studying Nursing because of the economic situation, I was already five years behind — so I got an intermediate degree, which was interrupted by my imprisonment during the dictatorship."

They were difficult times for the country and for the family. Tabaré remembers: "If you happened to live in the same bloc where a political prisoner lived, you were in serious trouble. Well, now imagine the trouble that the family of a political prisoner had to go through. I would visit Jorge in the Libertad Penitentiary (Freedom Penitentiary). It is paradoxical but that was its name. I was always very close to my brother — not only as brothers, but also as friends. So much that during my administration he was Assistant Secretary to the President and President of the National Drug Board."

Features of a Simple Man

The day of the interview with Tabaré Vázquez, we had the opportunity to follow his retinue by car to get to Government House with him and record the conversation. Some of the people involved in the production of the interview went by taxi, fearing they could be an inconvenience to the security forces that guard the presidential car. But there were no troubles. The official retinue consisted of three cars. There were no police motorcycles like in other countries, and the presidential car even stopped at the red lights. When we got to the seat of Government, Tabaré walked the streets like any other citizen, almost unguarded, and even received some comments from the occasional passer-by: "Tabaré! How are you doing?" Furthermore, the President of Uruguay allowed us to go into a cabinet meeting with our cameras, and that was quite surprising — it is odd to be there and shoot such situation in any other country. In that meeting, Vázquez and his Ministers were debating about how to carry out the transition to the Government of José Mujica, winner of the elections. Tabaré would tell me some hours later: "Here in Uruguay, they have always told us that during the first year in power it is not possible to govern because you have to prepare yourself and adapt; and during the last year in power you cannot govern because of the elections. So, out of five years you have, you can only use three. I rebelled against that possibility. I believe you have to work from the first year to the last. You have to work the whole five years.

Jorge's experience in prison also left the family some touching anecdotes. Tabaré recounts: "One day I went to visit my brother and the sub officer who received the visitors there must have not liked me very much. When they called me, I showed this officer my identification card and he told me: 'You will not get in'. I asked him why I was not going to get in. What was the problem? And he told me: 'Because your hair is long, and it is all over the collar of your shirt'. There was a girl behind me that told me: 'Look, I have a pair of scissors in my purse. Do you want me to cut your hair?' I said yes. She cut my hair and the sub officer let me in. Recently, during my campaign, I was in the interior of the country, and in a public appearance, a woman came to me and said: 'Do you remember me? I was the one who gave you those scissors so you could cut your hair and visit your brother'. Yes, this really happened."

When Jorge got out of prison, Tabaré was there to pick him up with his brother's son. Jorge remembers: "To meet again with the guys was beautiful — I have not seen them in so much time. It was a period of a very hard, very traumatic readjustment."

Years after, Jorge Vázquez talks about his brother with admiration. He says: "One of the things that impressed me — and everyone else — the most during his campaign was the level of trust that the people had placed in Tabaré. The people were broke and that process dealt exclusively with lifting their morale — making them regain the confidence. Tabaré always instilled the idea of 'Come on! We can do this!' That is one of the things I think that stand out the most about Tabaré."

The Doctor Goes into Politics

If Tabaré Vázquez always wanted to be a doctor, and he did (even while he was President of Uruguay), the question is, then, how did that doctor decided to go into politics? He recounts:

I was a member of the Socialist Party but I only did social work. For example, at the Progreso Athletic Club of La Teja, we started a community kitchen for children and a recreational centre for elderly people. We had several popular meals with another club we founded called El Arbolito (The Little Tree). We would help the workers that went on strike, that where setting camps, collecting food. And we also had a general hospital. I mean, my purpose was to do something social. In 1986, after the return of democracy, the Law on the Expiration of the Punitive Claims of the State was passed. We called that law the "impunity law" — it was an amnesty for the crimes of the dictatorship. Political and social actors got together to try to gather signatures to repeal the law. The Socialist Party asked me to be a part of that commission. I participated, we worked, and we got the signatures. It was there that I had my first political contact; until one day, when the 1989 elections were approaching, Frente Amplio (Broad Front) asked architect Mariano Arana to be the candidate for Mayor of Montevideo. Arana did not accept, and, as we knew each other, he proposed me as candidate for the party. At that time, we still had three months to the elections and I thought: "Well, if I agree to be the candidate for Mayor I help the Front and, anyways, I will not win," because it was practically impossible to win being so close to the elections. I said to myself: "I serve the Broad Front, I do not win, I go back to medicine and my political endeavours are done." But I miscalculated: we won.

Tabaré recalls the first sensation was joy and festivity, but then the fear came — and the weight of responsibility. He was worried because he had to put in practice what the Broad Front had planned for Montevideo. The victory was bittersweet for the doctor that was not a man of politics. Not just that, but what is more, he had never been at the Municipality of Montevideo. In a campaign act, Tabaré said: "When I take office in the Municipality of Montevideo on 1 March 1990…", but his assistants shouted at him: "You knucklehead, it is February fifth, not March first." Tabaré now tells me: "I did not even know when we were taking office."

There is a topic that marked that new member of the Uruguayan political class. The Broad Front talked about governing with decentralisation and with popular participation. Many intellectuals and theorists had made studies about decentralisation and it was a topic with great popular demand. So the candidate for the Municipality of Montevideo studied those topics and spoke about them in his speeches. When he took office, along with his administration, they were decided to satisfy the requests of the voters. Tabaré recounts: "We said: All right, now we are going to decentralise and we are going to give more participation to the people, because we have all this extraordinary theoretical development, perfectly done, perfectly thought out. But then, we all looked at each other, together with the directors of the Municipality who I had appointed, and asked ourselves: 'Decentralise how? When? Where? Why? What for? How do we do it from a practical point of view?' So we took the question out to the neighbourhoods of Montevideo. We would say: 'We are going to decentralise', and people would ask us: 'How? When? Where? Why? What for?' And, despite all the studies, we did not have any answer to those questions. So we generated a public discussion all throughout Montevideo about the political decentralisation — that is different to administrative or geographical decentralisation. In order to have political decentralisation you have to have a calling for sharing the power to govern with the people."

The result of these meetings and forums that took place all around the city was a project that Vázquez sent to the Department Junta of Montevideo in the form of a decree. According to Tabaré himself, it was a mistake. "I did not give room for Parliamentary political actors to participate in the discussion of the project. I created it only using what I had picked up from the people. So, I took the project back and created a commission where all the political parties that were at the Department Junta were represented. I asked them to create a decentralisation project. They did it — and a year later it was unanimously voted for. And up to this day, the decentralisation project and citizen participation project are still working. They need to be constantly improved, of course, but they are working."

Progressivism to Power
During the nineties, there was prejudice towards the left-wing sectors — they were thought to have very good ideas but to be inefficient to govern. The question to a progressive front that got to power with several left-wing elements is how they managed to break down such prejudice. Tabaré Vázquez analyses: "Prejudice is overcome with modesty, hard work and by working with the people. People must not be feared. Some colleagues would tell me: 'But we are going to go out to the neighbourhoods and they are going to ask us this and that and it is going to be a big mess'. I was certain that it would work because I believed — and believe — in the common sense of the people, in the intelligence of the citizens. We went out and talked to the people, and what did the people ask for? They asked for paved roads where there were dirt roads so that the ambulance could get there in the night. They asked for help in building communal centres so the people of the neighbourhood could have a place to celebrate sweet sixteen or weddings. They did not ask for castles or palaces or anything of the sort."

Tabaré adds that the leaders have to earn the trust of the people but to keep it practical. It is not possible to live in a constant state of deliberation — decisions have to be made. "When making a decision, you can be right or wrong," says Tabaré. "But when you listen to the people you will be wrong on fewer occasions."

One of Them

José Morgade, President of the Uruguayan Band of Street Musicians Union, says about Tabaré: "We found a mentor in him. He was one of the few professionals who got started working really hard. Tabaré Vázquez was a simple, humble person that got to where he is by his own means. No one gave him a leg up. He had to make sacrifices, so it is a double merit." Susana Silva, from the Arbolito Club from La Teja, recounts the day Tabaré graduated as a doctor: "When Tabaré got his degree, a little truck went from the Arbolito Club to wait for him at the university and brought him back. Since then, we started developing the little doctor's office in the club. And later, with Doctor Tabaré Vázquez, the 'Arbolito' Social and Sport Club Policlinic started."

After 170 years of Uruguayan history, when Tabaré got to power, he became the first President that did not come from the traditional parties. This created very high expectations in the minds of the people. How did Tabaré face this? He recounts: "I believe that the crucial thing to have in this situation is modesty. We have to know that we must learn many things because we had never been part of a departmental government and, of course, we had never been part of a national government. And, one thing is to prepare programmes and projects from the outside in case you get to government, and another thing is being in government. And you have to be very pragmatic: with your heart in the utopia but with your head and feet on the ground."

The conversation drifts towards Tabaré's definition of the model that the Broad Front has for Uruguay, and how it relates to the Latin American problems. Ultimately, he has to see which way of living is preferable for the Uruguayan people. Tabaré says:

Latin America is multi-ethnic, multicultural and has different political and historical aspects. And each country has its own distinctive feature, thus, there are no models that can be extrapolated from one Latin American country to another. I respect, for example, the Cuban Revolution, and I give it the credit it deserves, but its model is not applicable in Uruguay. "Che" Guevara said it when he was in Uruguay, in a speech at the University of the Republic. Uruguayans

Uruguay: Tabaré Vázquez

have a model for life that is different to the model for life that the Cubans have. And we cannot expect that the model that we have been carrying forward here — if it can be called a model at all — in Uruguay, in this left-wing government, could be extrapolated to Argentina, for example, or Brazil. Firstly, because we are a small country; and, secondly, because it is not possible to extrapolate a model from one country to another just like that. There is some common ground — that is true. The progressive thinking, for example, unites many of the Latin American governments. The idea of fighting for the most deprived. The Broad Front is the gathering of the traditional left-wing parties — like the Communist Party or the Socialist Party — worker union's movements, social movements and also political groups that had split from traditional parties. Therefore, this entire social and political phenomenon in Uruguay had to be put together in a front that established its characteristics, its rules, and its statutes, but also its political programme, its political project — a project that is not entirely left-wing, because some of the sectors that came from traditional parties are progressive but do not share the view of a fully socialist country. Thus, the Broad Front put this entire phenomenon together so it would adapt to the Uruguayan society, which is a particular one. I am not saying that it is better or worse than our brother countries' societies of the region — but it is indeed a particular one. Uruguay is an aged country in its structure, the pyramid is inverted: instead of having the young at the highest point, we have it upside down. Those of older age are the ones who hold the most important positions in this age group pyramid. It is a conservative country, a prudent country, and we have to adapt to these characteristics. We Uruguayans do not like adventure very much — we do not like it too much to the left nor too much to the right. And there is a very large political school that stays in the centre — left-centre I would say — and there is participation of some progressive right-wing sectors, and these make it possible for the model to be applied here in Uruguay — and I think these are the characteristics that the government programme and the political project of the Uruguayan left-wing have: a centre-left movement.

One of the subjects that the Latin American governments consider essential is the role of the State. I ask Tabaré Vázquez what was his opinion on this topic and he explains to me that the Broad Front encourages a better State and a better market. The question is then, how do you combine those elements? Tabaré answers: "We cannot ask the market for things it was not created to do. Neither can we ask the State to fulfil tasks that correspond to the market. For example, we are developing the 'Cardales Plan' which seeks to give triple play (internet, cable television and telephone) to every home in Uruguay. Well, we cannot ask for private companies to give these services to every home and carry out a social function. If we let the private companies do this job, they will develop a product, and only those who can afford it will get it. If, on the contrary, we would ask ANTEL — the national public communication company — to develop the project, it would not be able to do it because it lacks the economic and human resources to do it on its own. Then, what is it that we are looking for? The association between public and private so that the private part will fulfil the market function and provide the service but with a counterpart that will make sure that that service reaches to the poorer sectors. And ANTEL is the company that will regulate and make sure this project is carried out correctly."

Vázquez adds that you cannot ask the Uruguayan State to make armchairs or shirts or ties. But you can ask the State to make plans to deal with social emergencies or to make plans to safeguard the quality of the environment or ask it to participate in programmes for social justice and equality.

When he was Mayor of Montevideo, Tabaré had, on his desk, a list of the goals proposed by his programme, the Broad Front, and he would cross them out as he reached such goals. During his Presidency he did the same. An inescapable question is how many of those goals was he able to cross out. "We lowered poverty from 32 per cent to less than 20 per cent in five years. And if we carry on with these programmes, in five years' time, poverty is very likely to be down to less than 10 per cent. We lowered destitution a 50 per cent: from 4 to less than 2 per cent. I am sure that during the next period of government, with this political project there will be no destitution in Uruguay. We moved forward with regards to equality: salaries improved by 30 per cent, pensions went up and unemployment went down. We said that we were going to carry out a tax reform so the ones who have more would pay more and those who have less would pay less, and we made a tax reform that did just that. We reformed the health system and today we have a comprehensive national health system."

Vázquez is not ignorant of his accomplishments but he knows that one period is not enough to solve all the problems of the country. He mentions security, education and a better distribution of wealth as issues that need to be improved.

The Man and the Doctor

It is clear that Tabaré Vázquez true vocation is medicine. This was a controversial topic during his Presidency because he did not stop his labour as a doctor during his administration. But, what consequences did that decision have? Tabaré explains: "I was criticised a lot. They said: 'The Presidency has to be a full-time work'. I think it was a full-time work. They call me at any time — two in the morning, three, five in the afternoon, ten in the night — a Minister or whoever, and I am there. Now, there are presidents, in the global context, that have their hobbies and they do it during their presidential periods. There were presidents here in Uruguay that enjoyed playing tennis and two or three times a week they would play tennis. Others liked, for example, horse racing, and on Saturdays and Sundays they would go to the racetracks. Other presidents like to paint or write. Well, my hobby is medicine. I have always practised it and will continue to practise it."

What is medicine, ultimately, for this doctor that became President of Uruguay? In his own words: "I think, after forty years as a doctor, that medicine is like opium. You know it will do you harm in some occasions, but you have the habit and you cannot quit it. Medicine sometimes hurts the doctor and as the years go by and you become more sensible, the more you get hurt in some circumstances. Especially in our medical speciality where your hands are tied and you lack the resources to offer anything else than comforting, company, hope. But the exercise of medicine is really fascinating. For those who have the vocation, it is really priceless. I can stop being a politician, but I cannot stop being a doctor."

Tabaré makes an analogy between the political and medical exercise. He says that people trust a government in the same way they trust a doctor. The doctor gains the trust of his patients not only because of the knowledge he possesses but also because of his capacity to relate to the patient. Tabaré adds: "The patient needs to know that the doctor not only has the knowledge but he is also a human being and that he is not lying — even though he might sometimes be. Many times the patient will say: 'Doctor, I want you to tell me what is it that I have,' and he knows he has cancer but he is hoping that you tell him that he will be all right, even though he is not, because he needs that other fundamental element that is hope. And citizens need to have confidence and hope for a better future. But for that you need to earn their trust, so that it helps renew the hope in the sick person and also in the citizens."

Just as Tabaré Vázquez kept on practising medicine while he was in office, going back to his ordinary life does not only imply more time to dedicate to his patients — it also means, as he puts it, missing the intensity of work, his colleagues and the constant challenge to do things that will improve the lifestyle of his countrymen.

In addition, Tabaré wants to publish two books: "One for dissemination, to give elements to people to fight this cruel pathology that is the Mephistopheles of our times — cancer. The other one is a scientific publication in a bibliographical search about metastasis. Metastasis is that colony that emerges from a primary tumour and goes to other parts of the organism — and generally, it is this metastasis the cause of death of the patient. So, as you can see, I will be busy from 1 March 2010 onwards."

Venezuela: Hugo Chávez
A Chronicle from the Shooting Range

Hugo Rafael Chávez Frías was born on 8 July 1954 in Sabaneta, Barinas State, Venezuela. He was married twice and had five children. In 1975 he graduated from the Military Academy of Venezuela and was given the degree in Military Sciences and Arts, specialising in Terrestrial Communications. In 1977 we has named Communication Officer at the Centro de Operaciones Tácticas de San Mateo (Tactical Operations Centre of San Mateo) in the state of Anaoátegui. In 1982 he set up the Ejército Bolívariano Revolucionario 200 (Revolutionary Bolívarian Army 200). In 1991, he changed the name to Movimiento Bolívariano Revolucionario 200 (Revolutionary Bolívarian Movement 200). In 1997, he enrolled the Movement as a party. In 1998 he won the presidential elections and took up office in February 1999. In that same year, he called for a referendum to reform the constitution, and it voted positively. With the reform, he called for presidential elections again in 2000. He was re-elected in 2006 and again in the October 2012 presidential election. Chávez died on 5 March 2013 at the age of 58. Nicolás Maduro — who was chosen by Hugo Chávez as his successor — was elected President in April 2013.

The meeting with Hugo Chávez was going to take place in the Miraflores Palace, seat of the Venezuelan government, but the President decided to have it on the old Maracay shooting range. It is a huge field, surrounded by hills and with a tranquilising view. So, once we are set, the first question is certain: Why here and not in Miraflores? Chávez says: "Miraflores is like a prison to me — I am locked up between four walls. Of course, it is a very intense prison of forging and struggling. But here I feel free and also in touch with the roots. We are in Maracay, which means 'crossroad of every road'. Here is the Lake Tacarigua. This city means a lot to me."

What is the importance of this place to the President of Venezuela? What does it represent for him? Chávez continues: "I arrived here in December 1977. A few months earlier, I had been really close to leaving with a small group of soldiers towards the mountains of the Venezuelan East — because we were already an anti-guerrilla unit. But, there and then, I already knew that the ones who were right — or were closest to being right regarding the reasons for their struggle — were the armed rebels of 1960 and not us, who were chasing those who were fighting to liberate the country. Then, circumstances brought me here. Getting here got me away from the possibility of joining the guerrilla. If I would have stayed a few more months in the East, it was almost certain that I would have joined the guerrilla. I might have died. My life would have taken another course. So, I got here, I got married here, and I had my first daughter here — when she was born, I felt I was being born again. Here I stopped being a sub-lieutenant and was promoted to lieutenant and my military path was defined. In this shooting range where we are standing, one afternoon I got myself some already professional military comrades who had a progressive mind. Among them were Pedro Alastre López — son of an old guerrilla man that today is among our revolutionary lines — and Carlos Díaz Reyes — son of an old communist. We shared talks, and we read the *Communist Manifesto* by Marx, we read *What Is to Be Done?* by Lenin and we read Símon Bolívar. And in that moment we formed a first group, a first cell of what would become, in the next few years, the Bolívarian movement born in the quarters, in the shooting ranges, among troops, among soldiers. See what a seeming contradiction — but there is no contradiction at all because we are revolutionary soldiers. I come from, shall we say, a lineage of revolutionary soldiers. It is possible that in Argentina they see me with this uniform and this beret and they feel uncomfortable — especially in the South Cone — and it is understandable, but I belong to the side of the revolutionary soldiers. Who are our forefathers in arms? San Martín, Bolívar, Sucre. We are their children. We are their descendants."

As we speak, the night falls over Maracay. We need an electric generator to carry on with the interview, because where we are there is no electricity. As we wait for the light to come back, Chávez takes advantage of the time we have and tells us a story of adventure and intrigue: "They say that when Juan Vicente Gómez — the dictator who subordinated himself to the *gringos* — died, they buried a treasure in this hill. An old man used to live here — we called him *grandpa* — and he would tell us stories about how he had seen the treasure being buried. One time, Mayor Acalá — who was third commander of the battalion — found a golden coin (a *Morocota* coin) after it had been raining for a while and, then, a gold fever was unleashed in the battalion. I must confess that even I participated in the gold quest. Lieutenant Presuto Lauretti asked for a mine detector and we would go around with that metal detector. We found several snakes, but we never found Gómez's gold. There are many stories in this quarter. Do not be surprised if you hear things beyond the darkness."

The light comes back. The warm atmosphere lets us travel back in time and search for the trails of childhood of the President of the Bolívarian Republic of Venezuela. How was his childhood like? What were the things that marked him the most out of that moment of his life? Hugo Chávez recounts: "It was a very happy childhood. If I could be born again and I could choose the place, I would say: 'Dear God, send me to the same place', to the same little pitched roof palm house — unforgettable — the same earthen floor, adobe walls, a wooden cot and a mattress made of straw and foam rubber. A big patio, full of fruit trees, a loving grandmother, and a loving mother and father, brothers, and a little farmer's town by the river."

The memory gives Chávez the room to mention that in his family they were farmers, and from there he theorises about how to define the strata that exist in the society: "I do not like to talk about lower, middle and upper class anymore because I think that us revolutionaries must confront everything, including the codes of the small bourgeoisie and the paradigms they have imposed on us. Thus, I think we should march towards unity, towards 'a single class of individual', like Bolívar used to say — citizens. Now, I rather speak of lower income classes instead of lower class and upper class, because I find it offensive. Even if someone would talk to me about the lower class as the poorest, I would say to that person that that class is the upper class regarding dreams, love and hope. Among the rich people's upper class what abounds is selfishness, hatred and dehumanisation."

And reflection becomes family history: "So, we come from a family of deep indigenous and farmer roots. My grandmother's grandmother, who I got to meet, was an 'indian of the savannah' — as she would call herself. And my father's grandfather was a black man, and he was so black they would call him 'the African'. So that is where we come from: from that historical frame of the black people, the indigenous people and some of the white people. If you see my mother you will notice she is white. We have a white part that comes from our maternal grandfather. My grandmother would tell us about the darkness of the beginning of the century — it was the eclipse that they said would end the world. She would go on about that time when some comet was close to touching the Earth's tail, and if it would have touched it, the world would have come to an end in a great fire. Tales my grandmother used to tell."

When Hugo was a kid, they would call him Goofy because he had very big feet, like the Disney cartoon. People would also call him the *"arañero"* (the man of the spiders) because he would sell a candy called *arañitas* (little spiders) that were made of papaya. Chávez recounts: "My grandmother made those candies and I would participate in every step — I would get the fruit from the forest, bring it back at night, peal it, grind it really small, and then, in the mornings, I would go to school with a bag full of *arañitas*. I would sell them and we would have an income there. I would also sell fruits, oranges, yucca. We would take my father's bicycle and go get yucca from the big banana plantations that belonged to Antonio Guevara, a relative of ours through my mother's grandmother. He had banana plantations on the river bank — one could go there and get bananas and even sell them in other towns. I would go, for example, to where the men were playing bowling and yell: '*Arañitas* for sale!' Once I said: 'Hot *arañitas* for the old toothless *señoritas'*, but some people did not quite enjoy the verses I made up."

On those days, Hugo Chávez would get involved in grown ups' conversations and many times he heard about a murderer that had lived in the town. This is the story: "I would hear them talk about this murderer, and my godfather once told me: 'Look, Huguito, that man they are calling a murderer was your grandfather. He was not a murderer. Look into it because even in your family some say he was a murderer'. My family did not really talk about it. Inside my house no one would talk about that man. I grew up with that dilemma. And where could I possibly solve that issue? Here, in this quarter. I discovered that my grandfather, that some called a murderer, had actually been a revolutionary man — a revolutionary guerrilla man of the turn of the century, when the last riding men invaded these lands. Those were the days of Pancho Villa, Emiliano Zapata, Augusto César Sandino, Farabundo Martí. But here in Venezuela we also had our own riding men against the tyranny that the United States imposed in Latin America. One of those men was my grandfather. They called him 'Maisanta', the last man on a horse. I did my research. Here I hold his scapular which is more than a hundred years old. My grandfather used it in battle and died with it on. Nearby is a town called *Villa el Cura,* and there lives a ninety five years old daughter of my grandfather who I met being a lieutenant here. I started to investigate and I discovered the life of this grandfather — I was even imprisoned in Colombia because of my investigation, because of my quest. And I conquered my quest — it is the quest for the revolution. My grandfather, from the distance, made me more revolutionary and more of a soldier of this revolution."

Chávez's answers are long, thoughtful and full of information and reflections. It is hard to interrupt him. It is hard to break that hypnotic air that surrounds his discourse. That is why it is so easy to submerge yourself into another family story: "From my childhood I remember my grandmother the most. My grandmother was the one who was always there since you woke up — ever since I can remember. Our grandmother was the one that put us to sleep, made breakfast and cooked. She was the 'old mother'. The deep memory of my grandmother is stronger, deeper and far more eternal than the memory of any other person. Without discrediting my mother — who I love and is a woman full of courage. And without discrediting my father either — who taught me very important things and was a great role model. My father was governor of Barinas — our native land — up to a few months ago. Now he is retired. I saw him recently and he told me: 'I can no longer stand this retirement. I am off to the towns to give lectures', because he is a teacher. And that is how they called him in the towns: Teacher Hugo, with capital letters."

I am especially attracted to Chávez's parent's story because of their teaching vocation. I cannot help to ask him what impact it had on him, having parents who were teachers. The Venezuelan President analyses: "Maybe it should be inspected more deeply, but I think there is influence, no doubt about it. I have this image of me as a kid seeing my father in a humble classroom with desks and some students. I was not in school yet, but I would show up anyways. And I liked to scratch the blackboard with the remaining chalk and sit in those desks. I also remember that my father received a magazine at home called Tricolour, because of the flag's colours. As a kid, I learned to read with that magazine. It was a magazine that had a lot of traditionalism, a lot of folklore, a lot of culture, verses, coplas (four-line stanzas), drawings for children, explanations of what the country was, of the country's richness, of the national history. I started falling in love with history, with something they called 'Pages of History', which came with very good drawings. And it was there that I started reading about a certain Francisco de Miranda and Simón Bolívar. It is a magazine that we recovered recently because it had been privatised. We are publishing it again. So, there is no doubt that my father's vocation influenced me. I have always liked education and anything that can be considered a process of learning, of continuous education."

The Road of Dreams

Chávez's childhood was divided between two passions: arts and sports — or, to be more specific, painting and baseball. Little Hugo dreamt of becoming a painter and a major league player. This is his picture of his artistic dreams:

At some time I had reflected on what I have come to call the sequence of dreams that started to emerge from my heart. In Tricolour magazine there was a section called "Kids Collaborate" — children would send their drawings and they would put it in the magazine. I made a million drawings and I sent them all. Maybe they never got there, because it was in Caracas, and that was a whole other world to me — imagine this was in the sixties. And so, I started to grow fond of drawing. My father used to go to Caracas frequently and one time he brought home a Gillette encyclopaedia — a very good French encyclopaedia. It consisted of four books that to me were the whole world. It had art history, the history of culture, universal history, math courses — everything. It was a very practical encyclopaedia that made you work. Thanks to that encyclopaedia I started learning German. Then I continued with a drawing course. I started building an easel with chunks of wood. My grandmother would say: "This kid is going crazy. What is he inventing now?" She would always say that I was always inventing too many things. Then she would say I was an orchestrator — I was always orchestrating. When I became a military, she told me — several times: "No, my son, you are not good for that, you are an orchestrator. You will get in trouble... you invent too much." Well, she knew me very well. As a kid a built an easel with some nails after taking the encyclopaedia course, and I also started drawing following the course's instructions. I no longer painted by the book, with elaborated models — I painted nature. I learned about still life. One day my grandmother saw me with one of the few pewter dishes we had, and I was putting a tangerine on it, accommodating it, and she told me: "What are you inventing now?" And I told her: "Still life, grandma". "That is not still. You keep moving it," she would tell me. Well, I used to paint banana trees too — I can still paint by heart what I used to

147

paint as a child. One day I went out to the street to look for perspective. I could draw with almost perfect precision my grandmother's shack, which was an old house — a sort of emergency home. I could draw the fence, made up of planks of wood aligned one after the other. I could draw the branches of the tree that came out and cast shadows on the street. I painted. I mean, my first dream was to paint, to be a painter. And as an adolescent I still studied painting, but in the capital city by then. And I started to study the art of painting. I still paint, but I do not have that much time. I did not continue my studies, so you could say I am more of an amateur painter, a self-taught painter.

Hugo Chávez's other passion, baseball, also started when he was a kid. But unlike painting, this sport took him to some unexpected places. The President of Venezuela recounts:

When I was a kid, I already played baseball in Sabaneta City, but it was with a rubber ball and the bats were made of guava branches. I played baseball too at high school in Barinas. And I started getting better and better positions and I liked it. I felt I was good in sports — I liked to run and I was fast. They called me "roadrunner". I really liked that, I was passionate about it, and as I had stopped studying painting, I would leave school and go directly to the stadium that was some blocks away. That was my second dream — to be a baseball player. I was on my way. I took it seriously — I got manuals, I started studying the rotation theory of the ball. I studied and I practised. I even played national championships in 1969 or 1970 and I was not bad at all. Baseball passion was everything. I would jump of a plane without parachute for baseball. It was youthful passion. It was a dream that I lived with a great intensity.

Integrity
A neighbour of the Chávez family in Barinas shows us the house where the Venezuelan President grew up, and she recounts:

When Hugo was born, I was ten years old and we were really good friends with him and with his family and the boys — Adán, Aníbal, all of them. It was a very good friendship. They were very poor people. Hugo's father was a teacher, but back in those days, a teacher did not make much money. So their grandmother, who enjoyed making candy, would cook and her grandchildren would sell her candy. Their grandmother had integrity. She had character. And Hugo too. He has always been an upstanding boy.

This dream was fuelled by a tragedy. My hero was a young man called Isaías Chávez — he carried my last name but was not related. He was 22 years old and he had made it to the major leagues. They called him "The Whip", because when he pitched it was like a whiplash and everyone would say: "I want to be like Chávez The Whip". What happened one Sunday? I turned on the radio and I heard on the news that they were saying: "Last minute news: Airplane accident. A Viasa Aircraft, the Venezuelan airline, has just crushed in Maracaibo in the neighbourhood of Zaruma. No survivors, and among the passengers was the baseball player Chávez 'The Whip'". My world fell apart, as if a lightning had just struck me. I spent several days without going to school. I remember I draw The Whip's face and hanged it above my bed. I invented a prayer for him that I do not remember now and I promised myself I would follow The Whip's footsteps. But there is a key element there. We were very poor. My father did not have the resources to send me to the capital city to study. We did not have family in Caracas or Maracay or Valencia. I mention those cities because it was there where professional baseball was played. My father told me that they did not have enough to send me to those places and that I would have to go to Mérida, to a university in the Andes, where my brother Adán was already studying. I saw then that my destiny was Mérida, where there is no professional baseball. But one day, a lieutenant came to my high school to give a lecture. I arrived just in time and sat by my friends Jorge Ramírez, "Chelo" Rodríguez and Luis Reyes. I was interested by what the lieutenant had said. And I, seeking to get to those central cities where baseball was played professionally, went to enrol myself to the quarters of Barinas to take the exam in a fort in the outsides called Tabacare. I passed the exams but my father did not know anything about this. He did not oppose, but my mother did not want me to go. I insisted and went to Caracas. I took the exams, passed them and on 8 August 1971 — I remember it was a Sunday — I joined the Military Academy. My plan was to spend some months there and in November I was going to drop out, because it was not compulsory, it was voluntary. That was my plan. Make friends, find a place to stay in Caracas, look for a vacancy at some university and be closer to professional baseball. But when I first went to the shooting range, they put the rifle on my shoulder, a helmet and we would sing: "Oh, motherland, dear motherland, I am going to war to fight for you". We would also sing the national anthem, and I would look at the flag and remember my childhood, the Tricolour magazine and suddenly I thought: "This is what I am. I am a soldier."

Chávez, then, decided to become a soldier and not a baseball player. Did he ever regret that decision? Did he ever think his destiny might have been in the major leagues? He says: "No. I do not regret a thing. I am thankful to God and life itself. You see, one dream led me to another. And at the same time, that new dream took me to another. A few years ago, journalist Ignacio Ramonet told me that there was this rumour that I had entered the military as an infiltrator, because I was from the communist cells or the Che Guevara movement. That is just a big lie. They also said that I entered military school with a Che Guevara book under my arm. So I said to Ramonet: 'You can say that all of that is a lie, and what you can say is that four years later, on 5 July 1975, when I left the academy — a sub-lieutenant with a rifle at hand — then yes, I carried a book of Che Guevara under my arm. That is true.' I came out of military school converted in a revolutionary soldier. I was already in the lines of Bolívar. I already knew why one had to be a soldier and why one had to have a rifle. And that one had to play the game of History that was in full march. I had just turned twenty one, but I had already acquired a certain level of consciousness. So I left the military school with my eyes set in the horizon."

Hugo Chávez says he came out of Military School with a Che Guevara's book under his arm but, how did he come to read Marxist literature? How did he come to approach Fidel Castro's books and socialist books? It was like this: "It was in those adolescent years, when one has his first glimpses of life — a sort of awakening: your first girlfriend, more feasible dreams and that magical decade, the sixties. The Beatles, The Rolling Stones, May '68 in France. All of that was reaching us. Barinas, where I grew up, was, traditionally, a very cultured town. It always was a centre for poets, cultured people, historians, guerrilla men. So, in that cultured Barinas, of poets, I came across a great poet. His name was José Esteban Ruiz Guevara. We were neighbours. He also came from a farmer town and he was a grown up man, a family man. I became really close to his children. One was called Vladimir Illich Ruiz Tirado. The sister was Tania Marxlenin — not Marx Lenin, but Marxlenin, all together — so you can imagine how much of a communist was the old man. I frequently visited them and eventually I started talking to the old man. It was not easy getting to him — he would spend his days with a little typewriter in a little room full of books and newspapers. I slowly found my way into that room and I still have some of the books I took from that library. The first book I took was G. V. Plekhanov's *The Role of the Individual in History*. I devoured that book. I still have it."

Chávez tells me that he would go out dancing with Vladimir, Ruiz Guevara's son. They would meet this other Vladimir — Bustamante was his last name — and he was so radical he would say: 'I will dance with no girl until she defines herself ideologically.' Then Hugo would tell him: 'I do not have any problem; I am going to see if I dance with a bourgeois.' It was within that group that Chávez started reading the work of the revolutionary thinkers.

The Soldier in Power
A journal: that is the key to understanding how it is that Hugo Chávez — that soldier that wanted to be a baseball player and a painter — became President of Venezuela. When did it occur to Chávez that the governmental system needed to be changed? When did he see it necessary to get to power? He says: "A journal that I used to keep recently appeared in the hands of a woman that I loved very much and with whom I had a relationship of several years. She kept many documents of mine. In that journal I wrote one day: 'Today we ran a lot. I threw up in the field. I presented my math exams. In the afternoon we went to the yard to honour our new President. We waited like three hours. And he finally arrived.' The page goes something like that. That president was Carlos Andrés Pérez, who had recently come to power. It was 12 March 1974 — flag day, the day the president took office. And on that day I wrote: 'Someday I would like to be in charge of the Nation of the great Bolívar.' It was the first time I thought about being president — at least that I can remember. It happened when I saw a President coming towards us and we were honouring him."

Like a destiny — or history — paradox, that same man that awoken in Chávez the desire to become president was also the commander in chief when the uprising leaded by the current Venezuelan leader took place. In 1992, MRB200 (The Bolívarian Revolutionary Movement 200) attempted to overthrow Pérez. The coup, that Chávez leaded, failed, and he ended up in prison. He was in prison for two years until he was pardoned by the administration of Rafael Caldera. Hugo Chávez tells us more about that episode: "In this city I rose with my battalion one day, there, behind that corner" — he points to it — "there is where the old quarter is, my beloved quarter. I was there until 3 February 1992, the night we marched to Caracas through the highway." I ask him why he thinks that attempt failed. He answers: "It did not fail. We are here." I tell him that no, that in that moment the rebels could not get to power. Why? Chávez analyses: "If someone would make probabilistic calculations with a rational view, taking into account the different intervening factors, he would conclude that the probability of success was almost zero. I remember that Luis Reyes told me: 'Hugo, can't it wait a few months? The Air Force is not ready yet.' Other comrades from the Navy, from Puerto Cabello told me: 'Hugo Chávez, let's hold.' But it could not be hold — it was like childbirth. How do you stop a boy from coming to the world? But, from a strictly military and even political point of view, our chance, from 0 to 100, I would say it was 0.1. It was a truly quixotic act. We did not have any monetary support. The political parties that knew, the leaders, they all backed up at the last minute. There were supposed to be organised citizen groups, but they never came."

As is the case in many times during the interview, Chávez recounts an anecdote that includes his grandmother to reinforce his argument: "Do you know what my grandmother used to say? When on Saturdays or Fridays the day would start with pouring rain and I would have my baseball glove already on, I would say: 'Look! It is raining. The game will be off,' and I would get really angry. So she would tell me, quiet, sitting on her chair: 'Whatever happens is the best. You probably were going to lose, so if there is no game, you will not lose. Or maybe you were going to get hit in the head.' So, in 1992, I am convinced that what happened needed to happen as a necessary part of the revolutionary movement. There was no chance of winning there, but we left a hole in the wall. Like someone said: we hit the floating device of the ship with a missile."

Was he really filled by that optimistic thought on the day that followed the failed attempt or did he think that it had all been a failure? Hugo Chávez is forceful: "The next day I felt I was dead. I remember being in prison and seeing a priest come to me to bless me and lift me up. He told me: 'Get up, my son.' And I thought: 'My God. What have I done? What will be of my children now? I would say this as I lay on the floor, in a cold cell, in a basement in Caracas. They then brought me a newspaper where they showed the list of deceased from that day. I wanted to die. I felt like a living dead."

Seven years later, Hugo Chávez got to power through democratic elections. He got 56.5 per cent of the votes, fulfilling the dream of that young man that wanted to become a soldier of Bolívar. He became President of the Bolívarian Republic of Venezuela.

The Speech
Ten years had passed since Hugo Chávez got to power. In those times, one of the most widely known characteristic of him was his overwhelming oratory capacity. And here, in the old Maracay shooting range, I am a witness to such capacity. I asked him about that thing called "twenty-first Century Socialism". What ideological elements does it have? What influences? What distinctive feature does it have for being Latin American? What features differentiate it from traditional Socialism? Is it possible for that project to take place in only one country? Hugo Chávez gave his speech:

That question is life's dilemma, the challenge we face today. I have said that, to me, Christ had been a great socialist. I think that Bolívar had pro or pre socialist ideas in his thinking. Símon Rodríguez was a socialist for sure. I am talking about the roots of our rebellion that is no longer military. I am soldier, but no longer a rifle soldier. I am a soldier of ideas and struggles, of popular uprising — revolutionary and ideological. There is a deep Christian element, no doubt. But it is far from the limits of Christian fanaticism. Nothing of the sort. Christ, the man. I read a lot of Pierre Teilhard de Chardin when I was a cadet. A very good book reached my hands — *Evolution, Marxism and Christianity* was its name — and I understood thanks to Teilhard de Chardin that Christianity and Marxism can go hand in hand across the centuries. I became a Chardin Christian.

Antonio José de Sucre had pro-socialist ideas. There is a quote by Sucre that goes like this: "When the people of this America went into battle for independence, they also understood that they did it for justice and equality." Freedom and equality are inseparable. Sucre started handing lands to the natives and picking up poor children from the streets. He opened schools, he opened roads. Bolivia's first port — back when Bolivia had a sea outlet, because it once had one — was founded by Sucre and he named it La Mar, in honour of Marshal La Mar, a hero in Ayacucho. So, Bolívar had said it half a century before Karl Marx, and I think that he did it with more clarity. Simón Bolívar said: 'Nature makes us different as human beings; unequal — in temper, in character, in intelligence, in virtue.' But then came the State, the laws, education, arts and science, and put the human race in a state of equality that he called fictitious. It is political equality, social equality. Half a century after that, Karl Marx said that socialism needed to develop inequality instead of equality. We are not equals. I am not the same as you. A woman is not the same as a man. The Argentine is not the same as the Venezuelan. Socialism, Marx said, develops all natural inequality of human beings through a society that integrates them in a state of equality in diversity. It is as if Marx had read Bolívar. But socialism develops human beings with respect for their natural differences. Those who seek to equalise our thoughts, so that you and I will think the same, cannot do it, because it is impossible.

I think socialism does not come from the twentieth century — it comes from the first century, since the times of Jesus Christ. 'Blessed are you who are poor, for yours is the kingdom of God.' 'It is easier for a camel to go through the eye of a needle, than for a rich man to enter the kingdom of God.' 'Woe to you, scribes and Pharisees, hypocrites! For you clean the outside of the cup and of the dish, but inside they are full of robbery and self-indulgence.' Christ and his sermon at the mountain: 'Blessed the poor who mourn, for they shall be comforted.' 'Blessed are you who hunger now, for you shall be satisfied.' Christ in the temple with a whip throwing out the merchants. As a revolutionary, that is the Christ you follow. I think that socialism came from this. And before Christ, the prophet Isaiah: 'Woe to those who add house to house and join field to field until there is no more room and you alone are left in the land. Woe to them. They shall receive, someday, the whip of justice.'

Now, scientific socialism appears in the nineteenth century: Karl Marx and Friedrich Engels. And in the twentieth century, Lenin makes some theoretical and practical contributions. And many others like Rosa Luxemburg. And here in Latin America — our Latin America — after Bolívar, we have scientific socialism with José Carlos Mariátegui. And then Che Guevara and Fidel Castro. Ignacio Ramonet asks Fidel Castro: What mistakes did you make as you started the revolution? And Fidel tells him: 'A mistake I made, once the revolution was on, was to believe that someone knew how to build socialism.' Nobody knows. It is an invention. You have to invent it. Mariátegui said that our socialism — Latin American, Indigenous American — should not be a copy but a heroic creation. It must be created. One of the biggest mistakes of the twentieth century was trying to copy other models — for example, the Soviet Union. Che Guevara had already pointed this out in Algeria in 1963. He said that the Soviet Union would end in capitalism. The Soviet Union came down and not one worker stood up for it.

Twenty-first century socialism is a creation, but one that has to be created based on a doctrine and on scientific elements. It is as if you and I wanted to create a building made of water. Could that be possible? It could. It depends on the conditions, the temperature... but it is possible. Now, there are some key elements. If it is made of water, you are not going to use sand or straw. Then, we need to go through the doctrine of Historical Materialism, Dialectical Materialism, Class Struggle and all of what Karl Marx proposes in his thesis — Capital — about stages, about transition.

What is Socialism?
A man wearing a green shirt talks to us from his car about his own vision regarding socialism as proposed by Chávez:

Socialism is where equality exists. The poor man can have his own little enterprise, his microenterprise. We can all be equal, unlike capitalism, where the power lies only in the hands of the rich. Right now, with Chávez, there are quite a lot of cooperatives and microenterprises. There are good credits and a lot of assistance. The opposition is and has always been the little bourgeoisie, but they are only a few. What they do is to invent things and speak nonsense, but they are not the ones that are hungry. The opposition here is made up of rich men. The poor people support Chávez.

I think that, all in all, I see the socialist world in five fronts. I have a strategic line of thought influenced by the knowledge of the science of war. Now, Carl von Clausewitz said: "The war is a mere continuation of politics by other means". Well, if A is equal to B, then B is equal to A. I could say the same thing — that politics are a mere continuation of war by other means. So, I see five battle fronts against capitalism and in favour of socialism:

The first one — I think the most important one — is the moral and spiritual front. You do not become a socialist by decree. It is simple to say "Socialism, Motherland or Death; I am a socialist." Well, but the first thing is to examine: if some people have no conscience of the social duty, if some people are not capable of letting go of their egoism, of their personal interests, of themselves, then they are not socialists in its full dimension. If a trade union that calls itself "socialist" is not capable of fighting over more than just their own salary recognition and does not protest against the abuse that their fellow workers suffer in private companies, then they are selfish and not socialists. Thus, the moral battle is crucial. Then, that is the first front, the one that has to be mainstreamed — like they say nowadays — into all the other fronts. It has to spill and soak them all — like blood needs to get to the nail, because if not you lose it.

Another front is the political one. Democracy. But not the liberal bourgeois democracy but the protagonist democracy — the power of the people. There is a quote from the Hungarian philosopher István Mészáros that goes like this: "Socialist accomplishments ought to be measured by the degree of impact of its policies and we must value those accomplishments based on how much they displace the hierarchical social vision — or division — of labour, inherited from the capitalist model." In order to truly transcend the social division of labour, there ought to be truly democratic mechanisms of social control and general self-management. If this is not achieved, then socialism would be incomplete, like a table with just one leg. Socialism is democratic or it is not socialism. It is the power of the people. But bourgeois democracy is not. Let us not fall into that trap.

Then comes the economic front. The economic power needs to be democratised. We have to give the people the economic power. The means of production; the role of the State — mainly in the strategic sectors of the economy — ; a private sector that is subordinated to a general plan, to a Constitution, to laws and to a general interest. Capitalism's thesis is that of the free market. That is a fallacy, it does not exist. No market is free. It is just that they want to impose their thesis of the free market onto us. And that proposal for the FTAA (Free Trade Area of the Americas)... it was defeated and buried. The market is a reality, it cannot be denied. It would be like denying the moon, the night. Now, what type of market is desired? In a socialist model you have to tear apart, or tear down the created culture of a free market and an invisible hand that will make things right in the end — the biggest nonsense that has been said in centuries. No, the market has to be regulated, and not just with laws. It is the State that has to regulate. Now, that does not mean the bourgeois State. So then, what kind of State are we talking about? Here in Venezuela we are dismantling the old bourgeois State that was controlled by the bourgeoisie, the Yankee-lovers, and we have created a new State, a revolutionary State. And that is the reason for all the conflict. You can see it in the press of today, in the television of last night. It is a battle of every day. What is going on is that, up to recent years, the bourgeoisie did not pay taxes, the banks did not pay taxes. Nor did the big radio, newspaper or television networks and corporations. The big imports corporations did not pay customs duties — they did not pay any tax at all. They all lived from the petrol income. And there was a State whose Finance Ministers were subordinated to the bourgeoisie. The Finance Minister or the head of the Central Bank were appointed by the bourgeoisie, not even by the political parties. Now that has changed. Now they are appointed by a government that has no kind of commitment to the bourgeoisie. Who is the Finance Minister of my government? Ali Rodríguez Araque, communist, old guerrilla man, Marxist-Leninist. A humble and honest man, and a determined fighter. We can create a market that will include the private sector of Venezuela. A private sector that will be subordinated to the laws, and not the private sector that accumulates food to sell it at a higher price, not those who accumulate vehicles to re-sell them or those who contraband food to Colombia and the Caribbean. No. That is not market. That is not anything but mafia and criminals. Then: if you are a private producer and have a land here where you plant corn and cocoa; you have cattle and produce, and you have workers and respect their rights; you do not turn them into slaves; you pay them a fair salary, never below the established by the State; you pay them social security — in short, if you dignify them, you treat them like human beings and do not slave them, then you are welcome. In order for that to happen, there must be a revolutionary State. The Socialist State. And a Socialist market.

The fourth front would be the social one. A society of equals, in the Marxist sense and in the Bolívarian sense — a society where we are not equals but the society and the created conditions generate political equality, social equality and a socialist society where we all have the same rights and duties and where the ghastly social class division is eradicated. And, like Bolívar used to say, a moral society. A society in which Bolívar's words come true: 'Moral and lights are our basic needs.' A free country, an educated country.

And the fifth front is the one that is more difficult to explain. But I dare include it for debate. It is the territorial front. Territory. Some people think geography is a dead science that they forced us to study in high school. But geography is a living thing. What has more life than that mountain over there? Even though it seems not to move, it is alive. So, it is that thesis of radical geography. The radical geopolitics. Ezequiel Zamora said 150 years ago: 'Free land and men.' You cannot grasp time without space, for the love of God! You have to take space into account. That is the subject we have insisted so much on: the making up of a geopolitical centre, the integration between Buenos Aires and Caracas — to mention a South American example. But I can give an example regarding Venezuelan radical geography. We are now in the state of Aragua, that begins there in the coasts that face the Caribbean and it stretches all through this valley — the valley of Aragua. It passes the Tacarigua Lake and then goes deep into the heart of the savannah. It gets to the heart of it, it is a long state. Now, you must see the state of Aragua as part of a region, a sub region. You cannot grow socialism in Aragua without connecting it, for example, to the agrarian revolution in the state of Guárico. The agrarian lands must be connected with the industrial potential so as to push forward an agro-industrial revolution. That is to say, it is the vision of the territory.

There is also a sixth front that could be added that is the international front. The question is whether it is possible to have socialism in only one country of Latin America. I believe that it is impossible to have a revolutionary process in just one country. Some could say: 'Chávez is exporting the model,' but no, you cannot export that. That kind of thing grows. Venezuela has been under a siege;

Cuba has been under a siege for more than half a century. They have led it to a situation of extreme survival. Then the Venezuelan process emerged, in which, up to the year 2003, no one talked about socialism as a banner or a process. It was a Bolívarian revolution but it was not defined as socialist. The aggressions of the empire, the internal growth and the internal conflicts led us to take up the socialist banner as of 2003. We progressed and now we are a school of thought towards socialism. Now, we are aware that a process like this is impossible without international allies. And I do not mean a distant Soviet Union that no longer exists or a distant China — presently an ally and owner of its own model. No. I mean the geopolitical surroundings of Latin America and the Caribbean. It is a very Bolívarian concept. And it is here that Simón Bolívar takes on his most current idea. Bolívar said that "if we do not call for order and unity, our legacy for posterity will be a new colonial period". San Martín said: "Let's be free, the rest means nothing." Closer to these times, General Perón said: "The twenty-first century will find us united or dominated." And here we are, separated and dominated. We are uniting. Look how they attack our relationship with Argentina. The bourgeoisie here in Venezuela attacks it; the bourgeoisie in Argentina attacks it. The international sectors would love to break the indestructible bonds that tie the governments of Venezuela and Argentina together. The same thing happens with Brazil. Each of us is dedicated to their own project. It is well known that Brazil does not take up the socialist banner; neither does the Argentinian government. But we respect that. Each country has its own national projects, within their scope of possibilities and in their own field, with their own particularities. Correa takes up the banner of socialism of the twenty-first century and Bolívarianism. Evo Morales takes up twenty-first century socialism with an indigenous, autochthonous socialism. Daniel Ortega too. Fidel Castro and Raúl too. And something called ALBA is growing. It is the Alternativa Bolívariana para América (Bolívarian Alternative for America). It is a movement — a geopolitical, socialist environment of governments and countries that are emerging. And also of workers, because it is not made up of only presidents. Behind Daniel Ortega there is a people, a history. Behind Fidel and Raúl, well, I do not have to say much. Behind Correa, Evo, Manuel Zelaya — behind us is the people.

Hugo Chávez's discourse on twenty-first century socialism finished but the conversation continues.

Chávez Lives

Towards the end of the nineties, Hugo Chávez had already taken office and, in the region, some leaders that seemed to belong to another century still survived. He remembers it like this: "Among the right-wing presidents — that is to say all of them — I was an infiltrator. That thing was a choir of applauses to neoliberalism. And I was the ugly duckling — a cockroach in a dance of roosters. And, in the meetings, the South American presidents were all worried because Lula was doing well in the polls for the presidential elections. I would hear them say: 'Let's be careful. Lula might win.' They knew — and the United States knew — what was brewing in Latin America, mostly in South America. That is why I had a *coup* in my country."

On April 2002, Hugo Chávez was overthrown by the industrial business-man Pedro Carmona. Two days later, he was returned to power by the Armed Forces. The Venezuelan President remembers those hours: "The United States, with the help of several Latin American governments and transnational companies, had planned to finish me and this revolution that was just getting started. It was merely an attempt. It was like childbirth, a child that was being born, that was sticking out its head. They wanted to disappear me before Lula won the elections in Brazil. This city, Maracay, played a heroic role, together with the people of Caracas and many others. But here, the people went out to the streets and joined the paratroops. They raised their voices and so did the troops of the Turiamo base, where I was brought at midnight. They were going to execute me by firearm but the soldiers refused to kill me. And when I was ready, I remembered Che Guevara, the great Argentinian. It was past midnight, I was looking at a star, the sea was crushing in my back — the waves. I was with my back to the ocean and I saw a platoon coming. Everything was dark and I told myself: 'I am done. I am gone.' But I thought: 'They say that when Che Guevara was about to get killed, he stood up and he was all wounded. I am not wounded, I have an advantage.' Che stood up and said to his killer: 'Now shoot, so you can see how a man dies.' And I said: 'I have to die like this, standing. I cannot ask for mercy or be seen afraid.' I was ready to die. And in that darkness, at the edge of midnight, out of the darkness of the wooded hill, came some soldiers that did not know that the one standing there was Chávez. And suddenly the soldiers recognised that the person standing there was their president. So they got closer and one of them said: 'If you kill this man here, then we will all die.' I resuscitated right there, I was already dead. My death had been written. It was written in Washington."

When he finishes his chronicle, Chávez tells me that on that day he was able to carry out Fidel's order. I am not familiar with that story so I ask him to recount it. He does: "The night before, I was in the Palace, falling, sinking, and Fidel manages — I do not know how — to communicate with me. Cell-phones were not working; lines were collapsed. I do not know how Fidel did it, but he did. So, he told me: 'I do not know exactly what you are planning to do, but, Chávez, you are not Salvador Allende.' And he practically gave me an order. 'Chávez, you do not die today. Do what you must, but you do not die today. Here, your people wait for you,' he told me."

In recent years, Latin America has seen a process in which the countries of the region seek common goals, each of them with their own characteristics. It is a different process to that of the nineties because the goal now is to recover sovereignty and identity — two features that were lost, precisely, during the time of the neoliberal peak. It is a perspective that was impossible to imagine fifteen or twenty years ago. How do you construct such a quest? Chávez imagines: "I feel as much Venezuelan as I feel Argentinian, and I am sorry if an Argentinian may feel offended. But an Argentinian should also feel as much Venezuelan as he feels Argentinian, because it is all one Motherland or it is nothing. There is no space for small motherlands here."

In 2010, Venezuela, Argentina and other countries celebrate their bicentenary. Two hundred years after those glorious struggles to become sovereign nations, which are the pending matters that Latin America has to take care of? Chávez says: "Independence. That one gathers all of the others. If you tell me there are like a hundred, I will tell you that they are all tributaries to a river channel, which is the main, central and vital part: independence. José Martí said around 1780: 'The essential problem of independence did not lie in a change of forms but in change of spirit.' And when we speak about change of spirit it means a change of everything — and then hof forms. Also forms. Thus, we are far away from independence. Perón talked about a second independence. I have been a Peronist since a long time ago, but I rather speak of straight up independence because I do not think that it will be the second. Rethinking and searching deeply... It is the same one! It is the same blessed independence that we never had.

As if the clock did not matter, it has been hours since I started my conversation with the President of Venezuela. The meeting was coming to an end and I asked him what his dream is was. "Right now?" he asked. "Yes, right now," I insisted. Chávez thought and then said: "My dream is no longer mine, because, truly — this may seem a common place but I really feel this way — I do not belong to myself anymore. My life is no longer mine. I do not own anything. Here they accuse me of having a plan to stay in power eternally and concentrate the power, but I am not owner of my life, of my hours or of anything. But I do have a plan to let someone into power eternally: the people. And in that way end with the perpetuity of the power of the oligarchy that imposed itself at gunpoint using this uniform that I am wearing. So my dream is not mine, but it is to have a socialist motherland. What I dream about is a perpetual motherland, as Jorge Luis Borges said."

One of Hugo's daughters was listening carefully to the conversation, and besides her, Chávez's granddaughter. I asked him what he thought history would say about his administration. What did he think they will tell her granddaughter about her grandfather? Chávez says: "Well, my granddaughter is twelve years old and my children are all grown-ups. If it is for them, it is all right. They know who their grandfather is. They know who their father is. So I do not care much about that. But, to answer your question about how I would like to be remembered by history, I would say like San Martín: 'Let's be free, the rest and myself mean nothing.' I care about the motherland, freedom and socialism."

www.ingramcontent.com/pod-product-compliance
Lightning Source LLC
Chambersburg PA
CBHW050940050726
47592CB00007B/2377